THE
LIFE
OF THE
REV. JOHN NEWTON

WRITTEN BY HIMSELF TO A. D. 1763,

AND

CONTINUED TO HIS DEATH IN 1807,

BY REV. RICHARD CECIL.

BAKER BOOK HOUSE
Grand Rapids, Michigan

Reprinted 1978 by
Baker Book House
from the edition issued by the
American Tract Society

ISBN: 0-8010-2418-8

First printing, July 1978
Second printing, February 1981

PHOTOLITHOPRINTED BY CUSHING - MALLOY, INC.
ANN ARBOR, MICHIGAN, UNITED STATES OF AMERICA

CONTENTS

MR. NEWTON'S NARRATIVE OF HIMSELF, IN LETTERS
TO THE REV. T. HAWIES, PUBLISHED 1764

THE LIFE

OF THE

REV. JOHN NEWTON

Mr. Newton's Narrative of himself, in Letters to the Rev. T. Haweis
published in 1764

LETTER I

Introductory

I make no doubt but you have at times had pleasing reflections upon that promise made to the Israelites, in Deut. 8 : 2. They were then in the wilderness, surrounded with difficulties, which were greatly aggravated by their own distrust and perverseness: they had experienced a variety of dispensations, the design of which they could not as yet understand; they frequently lost sight of God's gracious purposes in their favor, and were much discouraged by reason of the way. To compose and animate their minds, Moses here suggests to them that there was a future happy time drawing near, when their journey and warfare should be finished; that they should soon be put in possession of the promised land, and have rest from all their fears and troubles; and then it would give them pleasure to look back upon what they now found so uneasy to bear: "Thou shalt remember all the way by which the Lord thy God led thee through this wilderness."

But the importance and comfort of these words is still greater, if we consider them, in a spiritual sense, as addressed to all who are passing through the wilderness of this world to a heavenly Canaan; who, by faith in the promises and power of God, are seeking an eternal rest in that kingdom which cannot be shaken. The hope of that glorious inheritance inspires us with some degree of courage and zeal to press forward to the place where Jesus has already entered as our forerunner; and when our eye is fixed upon him, we are more than conquerors over all that would withstand our progress. But we have not yet attained; we still feel the infirmities of a fallen nature: through the remains of ignorance and unbelief we often mistake the Lord's dealings with us, and are ready to complain; when, if we knew all, we should rather rejoice. But to us likewise there is a time coming when our warfare shall be accomplished, our views enlarged, and our light increased; then with what transports of adoration and love shall we look back upon the way by which the Lord

led us! We shall then see and acknowledge
that mercy and goodness directed every step;
we shall see, that, what our ignorance once called adversities and evils, were in reality blessings,
which we could not have done well without;
that nothing befell us without a cause; that no
trouble came upon us sooner, or pressed on us
more heavily, or continued longer than our case
required: in a word, that our many afflictions
were each in their place among the means employed by divine grace and wisdom, to bring us
to the possession of that exceeding and eternal
weight of glory which the Lord has prepared for
his people. And even in this imperfect state,
though we are seldom able to judge aright of our
present circumstances, yet if we look upon the
years of our past life, and compare the dispensations we have been brought through with the
frame of our minds under each successive period; if we consider how wonderfully one thing
has been connected with another, so that what
we now number amongst our great advantages,
perhaps, took their first rise from incidents
which we thought hardly worth our notice; and
that we have sometimes escaped the greatest
dangers that threatened us, not by any wisdom
or foresight of our own, but by the intervention
of circumstances which we neither desired nor
thought of: I say, when we compare and consi-

der these things by the light afforded us in the
Holy Scriptures, we may collect indisputable
proof from the narrow circle of our own concerns, that the wise and good providence of God
watches over his people from the earliest moment of their life; overrules and guards them
through all their wanderings in a state of ignorance, and leads them in a way that they know
not, till at length his providence and grace concur in those events and impressions which bring
them to the knowledge of him and themselves.

I am persuaded that every believer will, upon
due reflection, see enough in his own case to
confirm this remark; but not all in the same degree. The outward circumstances of many have
been uniform, they have known but little variety
in life; and, with respect to their inward change,
it has been effected in a secret way, unnoticed
by others, and almost unperceived by themselves. The Lord has spoken to them, not in
thunder and tempest; but with a still small voice
he has drawn them gradually to himself; so that,
though they have a happy assurance that they
know and love him, and are passed from death
unto life, yet of the precise time and manner
they can give little account. Others he seems to
select in order to show the exceeding riches of
his grace, and the greatness of his mighty power:
he suffers the natural rebellion and wickedness

of their hearts to have full scope : while sinners of less note are cut off with little warning, these are spared, though sinning with a high hand, and, as it were, studying their own destruction. At length, when all that knew them are perhaps ex pecting to hear that they are made signal instances of divine vengeance, the Lord (whose thoughts are high above ours, as the heavens are higher than the earth) is pleased to pluck them as brands out of the fire, and to make them monuments of his mercy, for the encouragement of others : they are, beyond expectation, convinced, pardoned and changed.

A case of this sort indicates a divine power no less than the creation of a world : it is evidently the Lord's doing, and it is marvellous in the eyes of all those who are not blinded by prejudice and unbelief.

Such was the persecuting Saul : his heart was full of enmity against *Jesus of Nazareth*, and therefore he persecuted and made havoc of his disciples.

He had been a terror to the church of Jerusalem, and was going to Damascus with the same views. He was yet breathing out threatenings and slaughter against all that loved the Lord Jesus. He thought little of the mischief he had hitherto done. He was engaged for the suppression of the whole sect ; and hurrying from house to house, from place to place, he carried menaces in his look, and repeated threatenings with every breath. Such was his spirit and temper when the Lord Jesus, whom he hated and opposed, checked him in the height of his rage, called this bitter persecutor to the honor of an apostle, and inspired him to preach, with great zeal and earnestness, that faith which he so lately labored to destroy.

Nor are we without remarkable displays of the same sovereign efficacious grace in our own times: I may particularly mention the instance of the late Colonel Gardiner. If any real satisfaction could be found in a sinful course, he would have met with it; for he pursued the experiment with all possible advantages. He was habituated to evil; and many uncommon, almost miraculous, deliverances made no impression upon him. Yet, *he* likewise was made willing in the day of God's power; and the bright example of his life, illustrated and diffused by the account of him published since his death, has afforded an occasion of much praise to God, and much comfort to his people.

After the mention of such names, can you permit me, sir, to add *my own?* If I do, it must be with a very humbling distinction. These once eminent sinners proved eminent christians: much had been forgiven them, they loved much. St.

Paul could say, " The grace bestowed upon me was not in vain; for I labored more abundantly than they all." Colonel Gardiner likewise was as a city set upon a hill, a burning and a shining light : the manner of his conversion was hardly more singular than the whole course of his conversation from that time to his death. Here, alas! the parallel greatly fails. It has not been thus with me. I must take deserved shame to myself, that I have made very unsuitable returns for what I have received. But, if the question is only concerning the patience and long-suffering of God, the wonderful interposition of his providence in favor of an unworthy sinner, the power of his grace in softening the hardest heart, and the riches of his mercy in pardoning the most enormous and aggravated transgressions ; in these respects I know no case more extraordinary than my own: and indeed most persons to whom I have related my story have thought it worthy of being preserved.

I never gave any succinct account, in writing, of the Lord's dealing with me, till very lately : for I was deterred, on the one hand, by the great difficulty of writing properly when *self* is concerned; on the other, by the ill use which persons of corrupt and perverse minds are often known to make of such instances. The Psalmist reminds us, that a reserve in these things is proper, when he says, " Come and hear, all ye *that fear God*, and I will declare what he hath done for my soul;" and our Lord cautions us not to " cast pearls before swine." The pearls of a christian are, perhaps, his choice experiences of the Lord's power and love in the concerns of his soul; and these should not be at all adventures made public, lest we give occasion to earthly and grovelling souls to profane what they cannot understand. These were the chief reasons of my backwardness; but a few weeks since I yielded to the judgment and request of a much-respected friend, and sent him a relation at large, in a series of eight letters. The event has been what I little expected : I wrote to one person ; but my letters have fallen into many hands : amongst others, I find they have reached your notice ; and, instead of blaming me for being too tedious and circumstantial, which was the fault I feared I had committed, you are pleased to desire a still more distinct detail. As you and others of my friends apprehend my compliance with this request may be attended with some good effect, may promote the pleasing work of praise to our adorable Redeemer, or confirm the faith of some or other of his people, I am willing to obey: I give up my own reasonings upon the inexpediency of so inconsiderable a person as myself adventuring in so public a point of view. If God may be glori-

fied on my behalf, and his children in any measure comforted or instructed by what I have to
declare of his goodness, I shall be satisfied; and
am content to leave all other possible consequences of this undertaking in his hands who
does all things well.

I must again have recourse to my memory, as
I retained no copies of the letters you saw. So
far as I can recollect, what I then wrote I will
relate; but shall not affect a needless variety of
phrase and manner, merely because those have
been already perused by many. I may, perhaps,
in some places, when repeating the same facts,
express myself in nearly the same words; yet I
propose, according to desire, to make this relation more explicit and particular than the former;
especially towards the close, which I wound up
hastily, lest my friend should be wearied. I hope
you will likewise excuse me, if I do not strictly
confine myself to narration, but now and then
intersperse such reflections as may offer while I
am writing; and though you have signified your
intentions of communicating what I send you to
others, I must not, on this account, affect a con-
ciseness and correctness, which is not my natural
talent, lest the whole should appear dry and constrained. I shall, therefore, if possible, think only
of you, and write with that confidence and freedom which your friendship and candor deserve

This sheet may stand as a preface; and I purpose, as far as I can, to intermit many other engagements, until I have completed the task you have assigned me. In the meantime I entreat the assistance of your prayers, that in this, and all my poor attempts, I may have a single eye to His glory who was pleased to call me out of horrid darkness into the marvellous light of his Gospel.

LETTER II

Early History to the Age of 17.—A. D. 1742

I can sometimes feel a pleasure in repeating the grateful acknowledgment of David, " O Lord, I am thy servant, the son of thine handmaid; thou hast loosed my bonds." The tender mercies of God toward me were manifested in the first moment of my life. I was born, as it were, in his house. My mother (as I have heard from many) was a pious, experienced christian: she was a dissenter, in communion with the late Dr. Jennings. I was her only child; and as she was of a weak constitution, and a retired temper, almost her

whole employment was the care of my education.
I have some faint remembrance of her care and
instructions. At a time when I could not be more
than three years of age, she herself taught me
English; and with so much success, (as I had
something of a forward turn,) that when I was
four years old I could read with propriety in any
common book that offered. She stored my memory, which was then very retentive, with many
valuable pieces, chapters and portions of Scripture, catechisms, hymns and poems. My temper
at that time seemed quite suitable to her wishes;
I had little inclination to the noisy sports of chil
dren, and was best pleased when in her company,
and always as willing to learn as she was to teach
me. How far the best education may fall short
of reaching the heart, will strongly appear in the
sequel of my history : yet I think, for the encouragement of pious parents to go on in the good
way of doing their part faithfully to form their
children's minds, I may properly propose myself
as an instance. Though in process of time I sinned away all the advantages of these early im-
,pressions, yet they were for a great while a restraint upon me; they returned again and again,
and it was very long before I could wholly shake
them off; and when the Lord at length opened my
eyes I found a great benefit from the recollection of them. Further, my dear mother, besides

the pains she took with me, often commended me, with many prayers and tears to God ; and I doubt not but I reap the fruits of these prayers to this hour.

My mother observed my early progress with peculiar pleasure, and intended, from the first, to bring me up with a view to the ministry, if it should please God to convert me by his grace, and incline my heart to the work. In my sixth year I began to learn Latin ; but before I had time to know much about it, the intended plan of my education was broken short. The Lord's designs were far beyond the views of an earthly parent : he was pleased to reserve me for unusual proof of his patience, providence and grace ; and therefore overruled the purpose of my friends, by depriving me of this excellent parent when I was something under seven years old. I was born the 24th of July, 1725, and she died the 11th of that month, 1732.

My father was then at sea : (he was a commander in the Mediterranean trade at that time :) he came home the following year, and soon after married again. Thus I passed into different hands. I was well treated in all other respects ; but the loss of my mother's instructions was not repaired. I was now permitted to mingle with careless and profane children, and soon began to learn their ways. Soon after my father's marriage I was sent to a boarding-school in Essex, where the imprudent severity of the master almost broke my spirit and relish for books. With him I forgot the first principles and rules of arithmetic, which my mother had taught me years before. I staid there two years: in the last of the two, a new usher coming, who observed and suited my temper, I took to the Latin with great eagerness; so that before I was ten years old I reached and maintained the first post in the second class, which in that school read Tully and Virgil. I believe I was pushed forward too fast, and therefore, not being grounded, I soon lost all I had learned; (for I left school in my tenth year;) and when I long afterward undertook the Latin language from books, I think I had little, if any, advantage from what I had learned before.

My father's second marriage was from a family in Essex; and when I was eleven years old he took me with him to sea. He was a man of remarkable good sense, and great knowledge of the world; he took great care of my morals, but could not supply my mother's part. Having been educated himself in Spain, he always observed an air of distance and severity in his carriage, which overawed and discouraged my spirit. I was always in fear when before him, and therefore he had the less influence. From that time to the year 1742, I made several voyages; but with considerable intervals between; which were chiefly spent in the country, excepting a few months in my fifteenth year, when I was placed upon a very advantageous prospect at Alicant in Spain. But my unsettled behavior, and impatience of restraint, rendered that design abortive.*

In this period my temper and conduct were exceedingly various. At school, or soon after, I had little concern about religion, and easily received very ill impressions. But I was often disturbed with convictions. I was fond of reading, from a child. Among other books, *Bennet's Christian Oratory* often came in my way; and though I understood but little of it, the course of life therein recommended appeared very desirable, and I was inclined to attempt it. I began to pray, to read the Scripture, and keep a sort of diary. I was presently religious in my own eyes; but, alas! this seeming goodness had no solid foundation, but passed away like a morning cloud, or the early dew. I was soon weary, gradually gave it up, and became worse than before. Instead of prayer, I learned to curse and blaspheme, and was exceedingly wicked when not under my pa-

* Mr. Newton elsewhere states that he went abcard his father's ship the day he was eleven years old, and made five voyages with him to the Mediterranean. His father left the sea in 1742, and in 1748 went as Governor of York Fort, in Hudson's Bay, where he died in the year 1750.

rent's view. All this was before I was twelve
years old. About this time I had a dangerous fall
from a horse : I was thrown, I believe, within a few
inches of a hedge-row newly cut down. I got no
hurt; but could not avoid taking notice of a gra
cious providence in my deliverance; for had I fallen
upon the stakes, I had inevitably been killed. My
conscience suggested to me the dreadful consequences, if, in such a state I had been summoned
to appear before God. I presently broke off from
my profane practices, and appeared quite altered.
But it was not long before I declined again. These
struggles between sin and conscience were often
repeated; but the consequence was, that every
relapse sunk me into still greater depths of wickedness. I was once roused by the loss of an intimate companion. We had agreed to go on board
a man-of-war; (I think it was on the Sabbath;)
but I providentially came too late; the boat was
overset, and he and several others were drowned.
I was invited to the funeral of my play-fellow,
and was exceedingly affected, to think that by a
delay of a few minutes (which had much displeased and angered me till I saw the event) my
life had been preserved. However, this likewise
was soon forgot. At another time, the perusal of
the *Family Instructor* put me upon a partial and
transient reformation. In brief, though I cannot
distinctly relate particulars, I think I took up and

laid aside a religious profession three or four different times before I was sixteen years of age; but all this while my heart was insincere. I often saw the necessity of religion as a means of escaping hell; but I loved sin, and was unwilling to forsake it. Instances of this, I can remember, were frequent. In the midst of all my forms, I was so strangely blind and stupid, that sometimes when I have been determined upon things which I knew were sinful, and contrary to my duty, I could not go on quietly till I had first despatched my ordinary task of prayer, in which I have grudged every moment of my time; and when this was finished, my conscience was in some measure pacified and I could rush into folly with little remorse.

My last reform was the most remarkable, both for degree and continuance. Of this period, at least of some part of it, I may say in the apostle's words, "After the straitest of our religion, I lived a Pharisee." I did every thing that might be expected from a person entirely ignorant of God's righteousness, and desirous to establish his own. I spent the greatest part of every day in reading the Scriptures, meditation and prayer I fasted often; I even abstained from all anima. food for three months; I would hardly answer a question for fear of speaking an idle word. I seemed to bemoan my former miscarriages very earnestly, sometimes with tears. In short, I became an ascetic, and endeavored, so far as my situation would permit, to renounce society, that I might avoid temptation. I continued in this serious mood (I cannot give it a higher title) for more than two years without any considerable breaking off: but it was a poor religion; it left me, in many respects, under the power of sin; and, so far as it prevailed, only tended to make me gloomy, stupid, unsociable and useless.

Such was the frame of my mind when I became acquainted with a work of Lord Shaftesbury's. I saw the second volume of his *Characteristics* in a petty shop at Middleburg, in Holland. The title allured me to buy it, and the style and manner gave me great pleasure in reading, especially the second piece, which his lordship, with great propriety, has entitled *A Rhapsody*. Nothing could be more suited to the romantic turn of my mind than the address of this pompous declamation. Of the design and tendency I was not aware: I thought the author a most religious person, and that I had only to follow him and be happy. Thus, with fine words and fair speeches, my simple heart was beguiled. This book was always in my hand: I read it till I could very nearly repeat the Rhapsody, word for word, from beginning to end. No immediate effect followed; but it operated like a slow poison, and prepared the way for all that followed.

This letter brings my history down to December, 1742. I was then lately returned from a voyage; and my father not intending me for the sea again, was thinking how to settle me in the world: but I had little life or spirit for business; I knew but little of men and things. I was fond of a visionary scheme of a contemplative life, a medley of religion, philosophy and indolence; and was quite averse to the thoughts of an industrious application to business. At length a merchant in Liverpool, an intimate friend of my father's, (to whom, as the instrument of God's goodness, I have since been chiefly indebted for all my earthly comforts,) proposed to send me for some years to Jamaica, and to charge himself with the care of my future fortune. I consented to this; and every thing was prepared for my voyage. I was upon the point of setting out the following week. In the meantime my father sent me on some business to a place a few miles beyond Maidstone, in Kent; and this little journey, which was to have been only for three or four days, occasioned a sudden and remarkable turn, which roused me from the habitual indolence I had contracted, and gave rise to the series of uncommon dispensations of which you desire a more particular account. So true it is, that "the way of man is not in himself; it is not in man that walketh to direct his steps."

LETTER III

Acquaintance with Mrs. Newton.—Voyage to Venice.—Im-
pressed for a Man-of-War.—1743 to 1745

A few days before my intended journey into
Kent, I received an invitation to visit a family in
that country. They were distant relations, but
very intimate friends of my dear mother. She
died in their house; but a coolness took place
upon my father's second marriage, and I had
heard nothing of them for many years. As my
road lay within half a mile of their house, I obtained my father's leave to call on them. I was,
however, very indifferent about it, and sometimes thought of passing on: however, I went.
I was known at first sight, before I could tell my
name, and met with the kindest reception, as the
child of a dear deceased friend. My friends had
two daughters. The eldest (as I understood
some years afterward) had been often considered by her mother and mine as a future wife for
me from the time of her birth. I know, indeed,
that intimate friends frequently amuse themselves with such distant prospects for their chil

dren, and that they miscarry much oftener than succeed. I do not say that my mother predicted what was to happen, yet there was something remarkable in the manner of its taking place. All intercourse between the families had been long broken off; I was going into a foreign country, and only called to pay a hasty visit; and this I should not have thought of, but for a message received just at that crisis, for I had not been invited at any time before. Thus the circumstances were precarious in the highest degree, and the event was as extraordinary. Almost at the first sight of this girl (for she was then under fourteen) I was impressed with an affection for her which never abated or lost its influence a single moment in my heart from that hour. In degree, it actually equalled all that the writers of romance have imagined; in duration it was unalterable. I soon lost all sense of religion, and became deaf to the remonstrances of conscience and prudence; but my regard for her was always the same; and I may perhaps venture to say, that none of the scenes of misery and wickedness I afterward experienced, ever banished her a single hour together from my waking thoughts, for the seven following years.

Give me leave, sir, to reflect a little upon this unexpected incident, and to consider its influence upon my future life, and how far it was subservient to the views of Divine Providence concerning me; which seem to have been twofold; that by being given up for a while to the consequences of my own wilfulness, and afterward reclaimed by a high hand, my case, so far as it should be known, might be both a warning and an encouragement to others.

In the first place, hardly any thing less than this violent and commanding passion would have been sufficient to awaken me from the dull melancholy habit I had contracted. I was almost a misanthrope, notwithstanding I so much admired the pictures of virtue and benevolence, as drawn by Lord Shaftesbury; but now my reluctance to active life was overpowered at once, and I was willing to be or to do any thing which might subserve the accomplishment of my wishes at some future time.

Farther, when I afterward made shipwreck of faith, hope and conscience, my love to this person was the only remaining principle which in any degree supplied their place; and the bare possibility of seeing her again was the only present and obvious means of restraining me from the most horrid designs against myself and others.

But then the ill effects it brought upon me counterbalanced these advantages. The interval usually styled *the time of courtship*, is indeed a

pleasing part of life, where there is a mutual af
fection, the consent of friends, a reasonable prospect as to settlement, and the whole is conduct-
ed in a prudential manner, and in subordination
to the will and fear of God. When things are
thus situated, it is a blessing to be susceptive of
the tender passions. But when these concomi-
tants are wanting, what we call *love*, is the most
tormenting passion in itself, and the most destructive in its *consequences* that can be named.
And they were all wanting in my case. I durst
not mention it to her friends, or to my own, nor
indeed, for a considerable time, to herself, as I
could make no proposals: it remained as a dark
fire, locked up in my own breast, which gave me
constant uneasiness. By introducing an idolatrous regard to a creature, it greatly weakened
my sense of religion, and made farther way for
the entrance of infidel principles; and though it
seemed to promise great things as an incentive
to diligence and activity in life, in reality it performed nothing. I often formed mighty projects
in my mind of what I would willingly do or suffer for the sake of her I loved; yet while I could
have her company I was incapable of forcing
myself away to improve opportunities that offered. Still less could it do in regulating my conduct. It did not prevent me from engaging in a
long train of excess and riot, utterly unworthy

the honorable pretensions I had formed. And though, through the wonderful interposition of Divine goodness, the maze of my follies was at length unravelled, and my wishes crowned in such a manner as overpaid my sufferings, yet I am sure I would not go through the same series of trouble again to possess all the treasures of both the Indies. I have enlarged more than I intended on this point, as perhaps these papers may be useful to caution others against indulging an ungovernable passion, by my painful experience. How often may such headstrong votaries be said " to sow the wind, and to reap the whirlwind!"

My heart being now fixed and riveted to a particular object, I considered every thing I was concerned with in a new light. I concluded it would be absolutely impossible to live at such a distance as Jamaica, for a term of four or five years; and therefore determined, at all events, that I would not go. I could not bear either to acquaint my father with the true reason, or to invent a false one; therefore, without giving any notice to him why I did so, I stayed three weeks, instead of three days, in Kent, till I thought (as it proved) the opportunity would be lost, and the ships sailed. I then returned to London. I had highly displeased my father by this disobedience; but he was more easily reconciled than I could have expected. In a little time I sailed with a friend of his to Venice. In this voyage I was exposed to the company and ill-example of the common sailors, among whom I ranked. Importunity and opportunity presenting every day, I once more began to relax from the sobriety and order which I had observed, in some degree, for more than two years. I was sometimes pierced with sharp convictions; but though I made a few faint efforts to stop, I at no time recovered from this declension, as I had done from several before: I did not indeed, as yet, turn out profligate: but I was making large strides toward a total apostacy from God. The most remarkable check and alarm I received (and, for what I know, the last) was by a dream, which made a very strong, though not abiding impression upon my mind.

The consideration of whom I am writing to, renders it needless for me either to enter upon a discussion of the nature of dreams in general, or to make an apology for recording my own. Those who acknowledge Scripture will allow that there have been monitory and supernatural dreams, evident communications from heaven, either directing or foretelling future events: and those who are acquainted with the history and experience of the people of God, are well assured that such intimations have not been totally with-

held in any period down to the present times.
Reason, far from contradicting this supposition,
strongly pleads for it, where the process of reasoning is rightly understood and carefully pursued. So that a late eminent writer, who I presume is not generally charged with enthusiasm,
undertakes to prove that the phenomenon of
dreaming is inexplicable at least, if not absolute
ly impossible, without taking in the agency and
intervention of spiritual beings, to us invisible.
For my own part, I can say, without scruple,
"The dream is certain, and the interpretation
thereof sure." I am sure I dreamed to the following effect; and I cannot doubt, from what I
have seen since, that it had a direct and easy
application to my own circumstances, to the
dangers in which I was about to plunge myself,
and to the unmerited deliverance and mercy
which God would be pleased to afford me in the
time of my distress.

Though I have written out a relation of this
dream more than once for others, it has happened that I never reserved a copy; but the principal incidents are so deeply engraven on my
memory, that I believe I am not liable to any
considerable variation in repeating the account.
The scene presented to my imagination was the
harbor of Venice, where we had lately been. I
thought it was night, and my watch upon the

deck; and that, as I was walking to and fro by myself, a person came to me, (I do not remember from whence,) and brought me a ring, with an express charge to keep it carefully: assuring me, that while I preserved that ring I should be happy and successful; but if I lost or parted with it, I must expect nothing but trouble and misery. I accepted the present and the terms willingly, not in the least doubting my own care to preserve it, and highly satisfied to have my happiness in my own keeping. I was engaged in these thoughts, when a second person came to me, and observing the ring on my finger, took occasion to ask me some questions concerning it. I readily told him its virtues; and his answer expressed a surprise at my weakness, in expecting such effects from a ring. I think he reasoned with me some time upon the impossibility of the thing; and at length urged me, in direct terms, to throw it away. At first I was shocked at the proposal; but his insinuations prevailed. I began to reason and doubt myself; and at last plucked it off my finger, and dropped it over the ship's side into the water; which it had no sooner touched, than I saw, the same instant, a terrible fire burst out from a range of the mountains, (a part of the Alps,) which appeared at some distance behind the city of Venice. I saw the hills as distinct as if awake, and they were all in

flames. I perceived, too late, my folly; and my
tempter, with an air of insult, informed me, that
all the mercy God had in reserve for me was
comprised in that ring which I had wilfully
thrown away. I understood that I must now go
with him to the burning mountains, and that all
the flames I saw were kindled upon my account.
I trembled, and was in a great agony; so that it
was surprising I did not then awake: but my
dream continued; and when I thought myself
upon the point of a constrained departure, and
stood, self-condemned, without plea or hope,
suddenly, either a third person, or the same who
brought the ring at first, came to me, (I am not
certain which,) and demanded the cause of my
grief. I told him the plain case, confessing that
I had ruined myself wilfully, and deserved no
pity. He blamed my rashness, and asked if I
should be wiser supposing I had my ring again?
I could hardly answer to this; for I thought it
was gone beyond recall. I believe, indeed, I had
not time to answer, before I saw this unexpected
friend go down under the water, just in the spot
where I had dropped it; and he soon returned,
bringing the ring with him. The moment he
came on board the flames in the mountains were
extinguished, and my seducer left me. Then was
"the prey taken from the hand of the mighty,
and the lawful captive delivered." My fears

were at an end, and with joy and gratitude I approached my kind deliverer to receive the ring again; but he refused to return it, and spoke to this effect: If you should be intrusted with th s ring again, you would very soon bring yourself into the same distress: you are not able to keep it; but I will preserve it for you, and, whenever it is needful, will produce it in your behalf."
Upon this I awoke in a state of mind not easy to be described: I could hardly eat, or sleep, or transact my necessary business, for two or three days. But the impression soon wore off, and in a little time I totally forgot it; and I think it hardly occurred to my mind again till several years afterward. It will appear, in the course of these papers, that a time came when I found myself in circumstances very nearly resembling those suggested by this extraordinary dream, when I stood helpless and hopeless upon the brink of an awful eternity; and I doubt not that, had the eyes of my mind been then opened, I should have seen my grand enemy, who had seduced me wilfully to renounce and cast away my religious profession, and to involve myself in the most complicated crimes, pleased with my agonies, and waiting for a permission to seize and bear away my soul to his place of torment. I should, perhaps, have seen likewise, that Jesus, whom I had persecuted and defied, rebuking the

adversary, challenging me for his own, as a brand
plucked out of the fire, and saying, "Deliver him
from going down to the pit: I have found a ran-
som." However, though I saw not these things,
I found the benefit: I obtained mercy. The Lord
answered for me in the day of my distress; and
blessed be his name, he who restored the ring,
(or what was signified by it,) vouchsafes to keep
it. O what an unspeakable comfort is this, that
I am not in my own keeping!—"The Lord is my
Shepherd." I have been enabled to trust my all
in his hands; and I know in whom I have believed. Satan still desires to have me, that he
might sift me as wheat; but my Savior has prayed for me, that my faith may not fail. Here is
my security and power; a bulwark against which
the gates of hell cannot prevail. But for this,
many a time and often (if possible) I should have
ruined myself since my first deliverance; nay, I
should fall, and stumble, and perish still, after all
that the Lord has done for me, if his faithfulness
were not engaged in my behalf, to be my sun
and shield even unto death. "Bless the Lord,
O my soul."

Nothing very remarkable occurred in the following part of that voyage. I returned home in
December, 1743, and soon after repeated my
visit to Kent, where I protracted my stay in the
same imprudent manner I had done before;

which again disappointed my father's designs in
my favor, and almost provoked him to disown
me. Before any thing suitable offered again, I
was impressed, (owing entirely to my own
thoughtless conduct, which was all of a piece,)
and put on board a tender: it was at a critical
juncture, when the French fleets were hovering
upon our coast, so that my father was unable to
procure my release. In a few days I was sent on
board the Harwich man-of-war, at the Nore: I
entered here upon quite a new scene of life, and
endured much hardship for about a month. My
father was then willing that I should remain in
the navy, as a war was daily expected, and procured me a recommendation to the captain, who
took me upon the quarter-deck as a midshipman.
I had now an easy life as to externals, and might
have gained respect; but my mind was unsettled,
and my behavior very indifferent. I here met
with companions who completed the ruin of my
principles; and though I affected to talk of virtue, and was not so outwardly abandoned as
afterward, yet my delight and habitual practice
was wickedness. My chief intimate was a person of exceeding good natural talents and much
observation; he was the greatest master of what
is called *the free-thinking scheme* I remember to
have met with, and knew how to insinuate his
sentiments in the most plausible way. And his

zeal was equal to his address: he could hardly have labored more in the cause if he had expected to gain heaven by it. Allow me to add, while I think of it, that this man, whom I honored as my master, and whose practice I adopted so eagerly, perished in the same way as I expected to have done. I have been told that he was overtaken in a voyage from Lisbon by a violent storm; the vessel and people escaped, but a great sea broke on board and swept him into eternity. Thus the Lord spares or punishes, according to his sovereign pleasure! But to return: I was fond of his company; and having myself a smattering of books, was eager enough to show my reading. He soon perceived my case, that I had not wholly broken through the restraints of conscience, and therefore did not shock me at first with too broad intimations of his design; he rather, as I thought, spoke favorably of religion; but when he had gained my confidence he began to speak plainer; and perceiving my ignorant attachment to the *characteristics*, he joined issue with me upon that book, and convinced me that I had never understood it. In a word, he so plied me with objections and arguments that my depraved heart was soon gained, and I entered into his plan with all my spirit. Thus, like an unwary sailor, who quits his port just before a rising storm, I renounced the hopes and comforts of the Gospel at the very time when every other comfort was about to fail me.

In December, 1744, the Harwich was in the Downs, bound to the East Indies. The captain gave me liberty to go on shore for a day; but without consulting prudence, or regarding consequences, I took horse, and following the dictates of my restless passion, I went to take a last leave of her I loved. I had little satisfaction in the interview, as I was sensible that I was taking pains to multiply my own troubles. The short time I could stay passed like a dream; and on New-Year's day, 1745, I took my leave to return to the ship. The captain was prevailed on to excuse my absence; but this rash step (especially as it was not the first liberty of the kind I had taken) highly displeased him, and lost me his favor, which I never recovered.

At length we sailed from Spithead with a very large fleet. We put into Torbay with a change of wind; but it returning fair again, we sailed the next day. Several of our fleet were lost in attempting to leave that place; but the following night the whole fleet was greatly endangered upon the coast of Cornwall by a storm from the southward. The darkness of the night, and the number of the vessels, occasioned much confusion and damage. Our ship, though several

times in imminent danger of being run down by
other vessels, escaped unhurt; but many suffered
much, particularly the Admiral. This occasioned
our putting back to Plymouth.

While we lay at Plymouth I heard that my
father, who had interest in some of the ships
lately lost, was come down to Torbay. He had
a connection at that time with the African Company. I thought if I could get to him, he might
easily introduce me into that service, which
would be better than pursuing a long, uncertain
voyage to the East Indies. It was a maxim with
me in those unhappy days, *never to deliberate:*
the thought hardly occurred to me but I was resolved to leave the ship at all events; I did so,
and in the wrongest manner possible. I was sent
one day in the boat to take care that none of the
people deserted; but I betrayed my trust, and
went off myself. I knew not what road to take,
and durst not ask for fear of being suspected;
yet having some general idea of the country, I
guessed right; and when I had travelled some
miles, I found, upon inquiry, that I was on the
road to Dartmouth. All went smoothly that day,
and part of the next; I walked apace, and expected to have been with my father in about two
hours, when I was met by a small party of sol-
diers. I could not avoid or deceive them. They
brought me back to Plymouth; I walked through

the streets guarded like a felon. My heart was full of indignation, shame and fear. I was confined two days in the guard-house, then sent on board my ship, kept a while in irons, then publicly stripped and whipped; after which I was degraded from my office, and all my former companions forbidden to show me the least favor, or even to speak to me. As midshipman, I had been entitled to some command, which (being sufficiently haughty and vain) I had not been backward to exert. I was now, in my turn, brought down to a level with the lowest, and exposed to the insults of all.

And, as my present situation was uncomfortable, my future prospects were still worse; the evils I suffered were likely to grow heavier every day. While my catastrophe was recent, the officers and my quondam brethren were something disposed to screen me from ill-usage; but during the little time I remained with them after ward, I found them cool very fast in their endeavors to protect me. Indeed, they could not avoid it without running a great risk of sharing with me; for the captain, though in general a humane man, who behaved very well to the ship's company, was almost implacable in his resentment when he had been greatly offended, and took several occasions to show himself so to me; and the voyage was expected to be (as it proved) for five years. Yet I think nothing I either felt or feared distressed me so much as to see myself thus forcibly torn away from the object of my affections under a great improbability of seeing her again, and a much greater of returning in such a manner as would give me hopes of seeing her mine. Thus I was as miserable on all hands as could well be imagined. My breast was filled with the most excruciating passions, eager desire, bitter rage and black despair. Every hour exposed me to some new insult and hardship, with no hope of relief or mitigation; no friend to take my part, or to listen to my complaint. Whether I looked inward or outward, I could perceive nothing but darkness and misery. I think no case, except that of a conscience wounded by the wrath of God, could be more dreadful than mine: I cannot express with what wishfulness and regret I cast my last looks upon the English shore: I kept my eyes fixed upon it till, the ship's distance increasing, it insensibly disappeared; and when I could see it no longer I was tempted to throw myself into the sea, which (according to the wicked system I had adopted) would put a period to all my sorrows at once. But the secret hand of God restrained me. Help me to praise him, dear sir, for his wonderful goodness to the most unworthy of all his creatures.

LETTER IV

Voyages to Madeira and Africa

Though I desired your instructions as to the manner and extent of these memoirs, I began to write before I received them, and had almost finished the preceding sheet when your favor of the 11th came to hand. I shall find another occasion to acknowledge my sense of your kind expressions of friendship, which I pray the Lord I may never give you cause to repent of or withdraw; at present I shall confine myself to what more particularly relates to the task assigned me. I shall obey you, sir, in taking notice of the little incidents you recall to my memory, and of others of the like nature, which, without your direction, I should have thought too trivial, and too much my own to deserve mentioning. When I began the eight letters I intended to say no more of myself than might be necessary to illustrate the wonders of Divine providence and grace in the leading turns of my life; but I account your judgment a sufficient warrant for enlarging my plan.

Amongst other things, you desired a more explicit account of the state and progress of my courtship, as it is usually phrased. This was the point in which I thought it especially became me to be very brief; but I submit to you; and this seems a proper place to resume it, by telling you how it stood at the time of my leaving England. When my inclinations first discovered themselves, both parties were so young that no one but myself considered it in a serious view. It served for tea-table talk amongst our friends; and nothing farther was expected from it. But afterward, when my passion seemed to have abiding effects, so that in an interval of two years it was not at all abated; and especially as it occasioned me to act without any regard to prudence or interest, or my father's designs; and as there was a coolness between him and the family, her parents began to consider it as a matter of consequence; and when I took my last leave of them, her mother, at the same time that she expressed the most tender affection for me, as if I had been her own child, told me, that, though she had no objections to make, upon a supposition that at a maturer age there should be a probability of our engaging upon a prudent prospect, yet as things then stood, she thought herself obliged to interfere; and therefore desired I would no more think of returning to their house, unless her daughter was from home, till such time as I could either prevail with myself entirely to give up my pretensions, or could assure her that I had my father's express consent to continue them. Much depended on Mrs. N——'s part in this affair; it was something difficult; but though she was young, gay, and quite unpractised in such matters, she was directed to a happy medium. A positive encouragement, or an absolute refusal, would have been attended with equal, though different disadvantages. But without much studying about it, I found her always upon her guard: she had penetration to see her absolute power over me, and prudence to make a proper use of it; she would neither understand my hints, nor give me room to come to a direct explanation. She has said since, that, from the first discovery of my regard, and long before the thought was agreeable to her, she had often an unaccountable impression upon her mind, that sooner or later she should be mine. Upon these terms we parted.

I now return to my voyage. During our passage to Madeira I was a prey to the most gloomy thoughts. Though I had well deserved all I met with, and the captain might have been justified if he had carried his resentment still farther; yet my pride at that time suggested that I had been grossly injured: and this so far wrought upon my wicked heart, that I actually formed designs against his life; and this was one reason

that made me willing to prolong my own. I was
sometimes divided between the two, not thinking
it practicable to effect both. The Lord had now,
to appearance, given me up to judicial hardness;
I was capable of any thing. I had not the least
fear of God before my eyes, nor (so far as I remember) the least sensibility of conscience. I
was possessed of so strong a spirit of delusion,
that I believed my own lie, and was firmly persuaded that after death I should cease to be. Yet
the Lord preserved me! Some intervals of sober
reflection would at times take place: when I
have chosen death rather than life, a ray of hope
would come in (though there was little probability for such a hope) that I should yet see better
days; that I might again return to England, and
have my wishes crowned, if I did not wilfully
throw myself away. In a word, my love to Mrs.
N—— was now the only restraint I had left.
Though I neither feared God nor regarded men,
I could not bear that *she* should think meanly of
me when I was dead. As, in the outward concerns of life, the weakest means are often employed by Divine Providence to produce great
effects, beyond their common influence, (as when
a disease, for instance, has been removed by a
fright,) so I found it then; this single thought,
which had not restrained me from a thousand
smaller evils, proved my only and effectual bar-

rier against the greatest and most fatal temptations. How long I could have supported this conflict, or what, humanly speaking, would have been the consequences of my continuing in that situation, I cannot say; but the Lord, whom I little thought of, knew my danger, and was providing for my deliverance.

Two things I had determined when at Plymouth; that I would *not* go to India, and that I *would* go to Guinea; and such, indeed, was the Lord's will concerning me; but they were to be accomplished in his way, and not in my own. We had been now at Madeira some time: the business of the fleet was completed, and we were to sail the following day. On that memorable morning I was late in bed, and had slept longer, but that one of the midshipmen (an old companion) came down, and, between jest and earnest, bade me rise; and as I did not immediately comply, he cut down the hammock, or bed, in which I lay; which forced me to dress myself. I was very angry, but durst not resent it. I was little aware how much his caprice affected me; and that this person, who had no design in what he did, was the messenger of God's providence. I said little, but went upon deck, where I that moment saw a man putting his clothes into a boat, who told me he was going to leave us. Upon inquiring, I was informed that two men, from a

Guinea ship which lay near us, had entered on board the Harwich, and that the commodore (Sir George Pocock) had ordered the captain to send two others in their room. My heart instantly burned like fire. I begged the boat might be detained a few minutes: I ran to the lieutenants, and entreated them to intercede with the captain that I might be dismissed. Upon this occasion, though I had been formerly upon ill terms with these officers, and had disobliged them all in their turns, they pitied my case, and appeared ready to serve me. The captain, who, when we were at Plymouth, had refused to exchange me, though at the request of Admiral Medly, was now easily prevailed on. I believe, in little more than half an hour from my being asleep in my bed I saw myself discharged, and safe on board another ship. This was one of the many critical turns of my life, in which the Lord was pleased to display his providence and care, by causing many unexpected circumstances to concur in almost an instant of time. These sudden opportunities were several times repeated; each of them brought me into an entire new scene of action, and they were usually delayed to almost the last moment in which they could have taken place.

The ship I went on board was bound to Sierra Leone, and the adjacent parts of what is called *the Windward Coast of Africa.* The commander,

I found, was acquainted with my father: he received me very kindly, and made fair professions of assistance, and I believe would have been my friend; but without making the least advantage of former mistakes and troubles, I pursued the same course; nay, if possible, I acted much worse. On board the Harwich, though my principles were totally corrupted, yet, as upon my first going there I was in some degree staid and serious, the remembrance of this made me ashamed of breaking out in that notorious manner I could otherwise have indulged. But now, entering amongst strangers, I could appear without disguise; and I well remember, that, while I was passing from the one ship to the other, this was one reason why I rejoiced in the exchange, and one reflection I made upon the occasion, namely, "that I now might be as abandoned as I pleased, without any control;" and from this time I was exceedingly vile indeed, little, if any thing, short of that animated description of an almost irrecoverable state, which we have in 2 Peter, 2 : 14. I not only sinned with a high hand myself, but made it my study to tempt and seduce others upon every occasion; nay, I eagerly sought occasion, sometimes to my own hazard and hurt. One natural consequence of this carriage was, a loss of the favor of my new captain; not that he was at all religious, or disliked my wickedness any further than it affected his interest, but I became careless and disobedient: I did not please him, because I did not intend it; and as he was a man of an odd temper likewise, we the more easily disagreed. Besides, I had a little of that unlucky wit, which can do little more than multiply troubles and enemies to its possessor; and, upon some imagined affront I made a song, in which I ridiculed his ship, his designs, and his person, and soon taught it to the whole ship's company. Such was the ungrateful return I made for his offers of friendship and protection. I had mentioned no names; but the allusion was plain; and he was no stranger either to the intention or the author. I shall say no more of this part of my story; let it be buried in eternal silence. But let me not be silent from the praise of that grace which could pardon, that blood which could expiate such sins as mine. Yea, " the Ethiopian may change his skin, and the leopard his spots," since I, who was the willing slave of every evil, possessed with a legion of unclean spirits, have been spared, and saved, and changed, to stand as a monument of his almighty power for ever.

Thus I went on for about six months, by which time the ship was preparing to leave the coast. A few days before she sailed the captain died. I was not upon much better terms with his mate who now succeeded to the command, and had, upon some occasion, treated me ill. I made no doubt but if I went with him to the West Indies he would put me on board a man-of-war; and this, from what I had known already, was more dreadful to me than death. To avoid it, I determined to remain in Africa; and amused myself with many golden dreams, that here I should find an opportunity of improving my fortune.

There are still upon that part of the coast a few white men settled, (and there were many more at the time I was first there,) whose business it was to purchase slaves, &c. in the rivers and country adjacent, and sell them to the ships at an advanced price. One of these, who at first landed, like myself, in indigent circumstances, had acquired considerable wealth: he had lately been in England, and was returning in the vessel I was in, of which he owned a quarter part. His example impressed me with hopes of the same success; and, upon condition of entering into his service, I obtained my discharge. I had not the precaution to make any terms, but trusted to his generosity. I received no compensation for my time on board the ship but a bill upon the owners in England, which was never paid, for they failed before my return. The day the vessel sailed I landed upon the island of Benanoes, with little more than the clothes upon my back, as if I had escaped shipwreck.

LETTER V

Sickness and Sufferings in Africa

There seems an important instruction, and of frequent use, in these words of our dear Lord, " Mine hour is not yet come." The two following years, of which I am now to give some account, will seem as an absolute blank in a very short life : but as the Lord's hour of grace was not yet come, I was to have still deeper experience of the dreadful state of the heart of man when left to itself. I have seen frequent cause since to admire the mercy of the Lord, in banishing me to those distant parts, and almost excluding me from human society, at a time when I was big with mischief, and, like one infected with a pestilence, was capable of spreading a taint wherever I went. Had my affairs taken a different turn, had I succeeded in my designs, and remained in England, my sad story would probably have been worse. Worse in myself, indeed, I could hardly have been ; but my wickedness would have had a greater scope ; I might have been very hurtful to others, and multiplied irreparable evils. But the Lord wisely placed me where I could do little harm. The few I had to converse with were too much like myself, and I was soon brought into such abject circumstances that I was too low to have any influence. I was rather shunned and despised than imitated ; there being few, even of the negroes themselves, (during the first year of my residence among them,) but thought themselves too good to speak to me. I was as yet an " outcast lying in my blood," Ezek. 16 : 6, and, to all appearance, exposed to perish. But the Lord beheld me with mercy. He did not strike me to hell, as I justly deserved ; " he passed by me when I was in my blood, and said unto me, Live." But the appointed time for the manifestation of his love, to cover all my iniquities with the robe of his righteousness, and to admit me to the privileges of his children, was not till long afterward ; yet even now he bade me *live ;* and I can only ascribe it to his secret upholding power, that what I suffered in a part of this interval did not bereave me either of my life or senses : yet, as by these sufferings the force of my evil example and inclination was lessened, I have reason to account them amongst my mercies.

It may not, perhaps, be amiss to digress for a few lines, and give you a very brief sketch of the geography of the circuit I was now confined to, especially as I may have frequent occasion to refer to places I shall now mention ; for my trade afterward, when the Lord gave me to see better days, was chiefly to the same places, and with the same persons, where and by whom I had been considered as upon a level with their meanest slaves. From Cape de Verd, the most western point of Africa, to Cape Mount, the whole coast is full of rivers; the principal are, Gambia, Rio Grande, Sierra Leone, and Sherbro. Of the former, as it is well known, and I was never there, I need say nothing. The Rio Grande (like the Nile) divides into many branches near the sea. On the most northerly, called *Cacheo*, the Portuguese have a settlement. The most southern branch, known by the name of *Rio Nuna*, is, or then was, the usual boundary of the white men's trade northward. Sierra Leone is a mountainous peninsula, uninhabited, and, I believe, inaccessible, upon account of the thick woods, excepting those parts which lie near the water. The river is large and navigable. From hence, about twelve leagues to the south-east, are three contiguous islands, called the *Benanoes*, about twenty miles in circuit; this was about the centre of the white men's residence. Seven leagues farther, the same way, lie the Plantanes, three small islands, two miles distant from the continent at the point, which forms one side of the Sherbro. This river is more properly a *sound*, running within a long island, and receiving the confluence of several large rivers, "*rivers unknown to song*," but far

more deeply engraven in my remembrance than
the Po or Tiber. The southernmost of these has
a very peculiar course, almost parallel to the
coast ; so that in tracing it a great many leagues
upward, it will seldom lead one above three miles,
and sometimes not more than half a mile from
the sea-shore. Indeed, I know not but that all
these rivers may have communications with each
other, and with the sea in many places, which I
have not remarked. If you cast your eyes upon
a large map of Africa while you are reading this,
you will have a general idea of the country I was
in : for though the maps are very incorrect, most
of the places I have mentioned are inserted, and
in the same order as I have named them.

My new master had formerly resided near
Cape Mount, but now he settled at the Plantanes,
upon the largest of the three islands. It is a low
sandy island, about two miles in circumference,
and almost covered with palm-trees. We immediately began to build a house, and to enter upon
trade. I had now some desire to retrieve my
lost time, and to exert diligence in what was be
fore me ; and he was a man with whom I might
have lived tolerably well, if he had not been soon
influenced against me : but he was much under
the direction of a black woman who lived with
him as a wife. She was a person of some conse
quence in her own country, and he owed his first

rise to her interest. This woman (I know not for what reason) was strangely prejudiced against me from the first; and what made it still worse for me, was a severe fit of illness, which attacked me very soon, before I had opportunity to show what I could or would do in his service. I was sick when he sailed in a shallop to Rio Nuna, and he left me in her hands. At first I was taken some care of; but as I did not recover very soon, she grew weary, and entirely neglected me. I had sometimes not a little difficulty to procure a draught of cold water when burning with a fever. My bed was a mat spread upon a board or chest, and a log of wood my pillow. When my fever left me, and appetite returned, I would gladly have eaten, but there was no one gave unto me. She lived in plenty herself, but hardly allowed me sufficient to sustain life, except now and then, when in the highest good humor, she would send me victuals in her own plate after she had dined; and this (so greatly was my pride humbled) I received with thanks and eagerness, as the most needy beggar does an alms. Once, I well remember, I was called to receive this bounty from her own hand; but being exceeding weak and feeble, I dropped the plate. Those who live in plenty can hardly conceive how this loss touched me; but she had the cruelty to laugh at my disappointment; and, though the table was covered with dishes, (for she lived much in the European manner,) she refused to give me any more. My distress has been at times so great as to compel me to go by night and pull up roots in the plantation, (though at the risk of being punished as a thief,) which I have eaten raw upon the spot for fear of discovery. The roots I speak of are very wholesome food when boiled or roasted; but as unfit to be eaten raw, in any quantity, as a potatoe. The consequence of this diet, which, after the first experiment, I always expected, and seldom missed, was the same as if I had taken *tartar emetic;* so that I have often returned as empty as I went; yet necessity urged me to repeat the trial several times. I have sometimes been relieved by strangers; nay, even by the slaves in the chain, who have secretly brought me victuals (for they durst not be seen to do it) from their own slender pittance. Next to pressing want, nothing sits harder upon the mind than *scorn* and *contempt;* and of this, likewise, I had an abundant measure. When I was very slowly recovering, this woman would sometimes pay me a visit, not to pity or relieve, but to insult me. She would call me worthless and indolent, and compel me to walk; which, when I could hardly do, she would set her attendants to mimic my motion, to clap their hands, laugh, and throw limes at me; or, if they chose, to throw stones; (as I think was the case once or twice;) they were not rebuked; but, in general, though all who depended on her favor must join in her treatment, yet, when she was out of sight I was rather pitied than scorned by the meanest of her slaves. At length my master returned from his voyage. I complained of ill-usage; but he could not believe me; and as I did it in her hearing, I fared no better for it. But in his second voyage he took me with him. We did pretty well for awhile, till a brother-trader he met in the river persuaded him that I was unfaithful, and stole his goods in the night, or when he was on shore. This was almost the only vice I could not be justly charged with: the only remains of a good education I could boast of was what is commonly called *honesty;* and, as far as he had entrusted me, I had been always faithful; and though my great distress might, in some measure, have excused me, I never once thought of defrauding him in the smallest matter. However, the charge was believed, and I was condemned without evidence. From that time he likewise used me very hardly: whenever he left the vessel I was locked upon deck, with a pint of rice for my day's allowance; and if he staid longer, I had no relief till his return. Indeed, I believe I should have been nearly starved, but for an opportunity of catching fish sometimes. When fowls were killed for his own use I seldom was allowed any part but the entrails, to bait my hooks with : and at what we call *slack water*, that is, about the changing of the tides, when the current was still, I used generally to fish, (for at other times it was not practicable,) and I very often succeeded. If I saw a fish upon my hook, my joy was little less than any other person may have found in the accomplishment of the scheme he had most at heart. Such a fish, hastily broiled, or rather half burnt, without sauce, salt or bread, has afforded me a delicious meal. If I caught none, I might (if I could) sleep away my hunger till the next return of slack water, and then try again. Nor did I suffer less from the inclemency of the weather and the want of clothes. The rainy season was now advancing ; my whole suit was a shirt, a pair of trowsers, a cotton handkerchief instead of a cap, and a cotton cloth about two yards long, to supply the want of upper garments ; and thus accoutred, I have been exposed for twenty, thirty, perhaps nearly forty hours together, in incessant rains, accompanied with strong gales of wind, without the least shelter, when my master was on shore. I feel, to this day, some faint returns of the violent pains I then contracted. The excessive cold and wet I endured in that voyage, and so soon after I had recovered from a long sickness, quite broke my constitution and my spirits. The latter were soon restored; but the effects of the former still remain with me as a needful *memento* of the service and wages of sin.

In about two months we returned, and then the rest of the time I remained with him was chiefly spent at the Plantanes, under the same regimen as I have already mentioned. My haughty heart was now brought down; not to a wholesome repentance, nor to the language of the prodigal: this was far from me; but my spirits were sunk; I lost all resolution, and almost all reflection. I had lost the fierceness which fired me on board the Harwich, and which made me capable of the most desperate attempts; but I was no farther changed than a tiger tamed by hunger; remove the occasion, and he will be as wild as ever.

One thing, though strange, is most true Though destitute of food and clothing, depressed to a degree beyond common wretchedness, I could sometimes collect my mind to mathematical studies. I had bought *Barrow's Euclid* at Plymouth; it was the only volume I brought on shore; it was always with me, and I used to take it to remote corners of the island, by the sea-side, and drew my *diagrams* with a long stick upon the sand. Thus I often beguiled my sorrows, and almost forgot my feelings: and thus, without any other assistance, I made myself, in a good measure, master of the first six books of *Euclid*.

~~~~~~~~~~~~~~~~~~~~~~~~~~~~

LETTER VI

Continuance in Africa.—Is sent for by his Father, and embarks for England, 1747

There is much piety and spirit in the grateful acknowledgment of Jacob, "With my staff I passed over this Jordan, and now I am become two bands." These are words which ought to affect me with a peculiar emotion. I remember that some of those mournful days to which my last letter refers, I was busied in planting some *lime* or *lemon-trees*. The plants I put in the ground were no longer than a young gooseberry-bush; my master and his mistress passing by the place, stopped a while to look at me: at last, "Who knows," says he, "who knows, but by the time these trees grow up and bear, you may go home to England, obtain the command of a ship, and return to reap the fruits of your labors? We see strange things sometimes happen." This, as he intended it, was a cutting sarcasm. I believe he thought it full as probable that I should live to be king of Poland. Yet it proved a prediction, and they (one of them at least) lived to see me return from England in the capacity he had mentioned, and pluck some of the first limes from those very trees. How can I proceed in my relation, till I raise a monument to the Divine goodness, by comparing the circumstances in which the Lord has since placed me with what I was at that time! Had you seen me, sir, then go, pensive and solitary, in the dead of night, to wash my one shirt upon the rocks, and afterward put it on wet, that it might dry upon my back while I slept; had you seen me so poor a figure, that when a ship's boat came to the island shame often constrained me to hide myself in the woods from the sight of strangers: especially had you known that my conduct, principles and heart were still darker than my outward condition; how little would you have imagined that one who so fully answered to the description of the apostle, "hateful, and hating one another," was reserved to be so peculiar an instance of the providential care and exuberant goodness of God! There was, at that time, but one earnest desire in my heart, which was not contrary and shocking both to religion and reason: that *one* desire, though my

vile licentious life rendered me peculiarly unworthy of success, and though a thousand difficulties seemed to render it impossible, the Lord
was pleased to gratify. But this favor, though
great, and greatly prized, was a small thing,
compared to the blessings of his grace: he
spared me, to give me " the knowledge of himself in the person of Jesus Christ." In love to
my soul he delivered me from the pit of corrup-
tion, and cast all my aggravated sins behind his
back. He brought my feet into the paths of
peace. This is, indeed, the chief article, but it
is not the whole. When he made me acceptable
to himself in the Beloved, he gave me favor in
the sight of others. He raised me new friends,
protected and guided me through a long series
of dangers, and crowned every day with repeated mercies. To him I owe it that I am still alive,
and that I am not still living in hunger, and in
thirst, and in nakedness, and the want of all
things: into that state I brought myself; but
it was He who delivered me. He has given me
an easy situation in life, some experimental
knowledge of his Gospel, a large acquaintance
among his people, a friendship and correspondence with several of his most honored servants.
But it is as difficult to enumerate my present advantages, as it is fully to describe the evils and
miseries of the preceding contrast.

I know not exactly how long things continued with me thus, but I believe nearly a twelvemonth. In this interval I wrote two or three times to my father: I gave him an account of my condition, and desired his assistance; intimating at the same time, that I had resolved not to return to England unless he was pleased to send for me. I have likewise by me letters written to Mrs. N—— in that dismal period: so that at the lowest ebb, it seems I still retained a hope of seeing her again. My father applied to his friend in Liverpool, of whom I have spoken before; who gave orders accordingly, to a captain of his who was then fitting out for Gambia and Sierra Leone.

Some time within the year, as I have said, I obtained my master's consent to live with another trader who dwelt upon the same island. Without his consent I could not be taken; and he was unwilling to do it sooner; but it was then brought about. This was an alteration much to my advantage: I was soon decently clothed, lived in plenty, was considered as a companion, and trusted with the care of all his domestic effects, which were to the amount of some thousand pounds. This man had several factories and white servants in different places; particularly one in Kittam, the river I spoke of, which runs so nearly along the sea-cost. I was soon appointed to go there, where I had a share in the management of business jointly with another of his servants. We lived as we pleased, business flourished, and our employer was satisfied. Here I began to be wretch enough to think myself *happy*. There is a significant phrase frequently used in those parts, That such a white man has grown *black*. It does not intend an alteration of complexion, but disposition. I have known several who, settling in Africa after the age of thirty or forty, have, at that time of life, been gradually assimilated to the tempers, customs and ceremonies of the natives, so far as to prefer that country to England: they have even become dupes to all the pretended charms, necromancies, amulets and divinations of the blinded negroes, and put more trust in such things than the wiser sort among the natives. A part of this spirit of infatuation was growing upon me; (in time, perhaps, I might have yielded to the whole;) I entered into closer engagements with the inhabitants; and should have lived and died a wretch amongst them, if the Lord had not watched over me for good. Not that I had lost those ideas which chiefly engaged my heart to England; but despair of seeing them accomplished made me willing to remain where I was. I thought I could more easily bear the disappointment in this situation than nearer home. But as soon as I had fixed my connections and plans with these views, the Lord providentially interposed to break them in pieces, and to save me from ruin in spite of myself.

In the meantime the ship that had orders to bring me home arrived at Sierra Leone. The captain made inquiry for me there, and at the Benanoes; but understanding that I was at a great distance in the country, he thought no more about me. Without doubt, the hand of God directed my being placed at Kittam just at this time; for, as the ship came no nearer than the Benanoes, and staid but a few days, if I had been at the Plantanes I could not perhaps have heard of her till she had sailed. The same must have certainly been the event had I been sent to any other factory, of which my new master had several upon different rivers. But though the place I was at was a long way up a river, much more than a hundred miles distance from the Plantanes, yet, by the peculiar situation which I have already noticed, I was still within a mile of the sea-coast. To make the interposition more remarkable, I was at that very juncture going in quest of trade to a place at some distance directly from the sea; and should have set out a day or two before, but that we waited for a few articles from the next ship that offered, to complete the assortment of goods I was to take with me. We used sometimes to walk on the beach, in expectation of seeing a vessel pass by; but this was very precarious, as at that time the place was not at all resorted to by ships for trade. Many passed in the night, others kept at a considerable distance from the shore. In a word, I do not know that any one had stopped while I was there, though some had before, upon observing a signal made from the shore. In February, 1747, (I know not the exact day,) my fellow-servant walking down on the beach in the forenoon, saw a vessel sailing past, and made a smoke in token of trade. She was already a little beyond the place; and as the wind was fair the captain was in some demur whether to stop or not. However, had my companion been half an hour later she would have been gone beyond recall; but he soon saw her come to an anchor, and went on board in a canoe; and this proved the very ship I have spoken of. One of the first questions he was asked was concerning me; and when the captain understood I was so near, he came on shore to deliver his message. Had an invitation from home reached me when I was sick and starving at the Plantanes I should have received it as life from the dead; but now, for the reasons already given, I heard it at first with indifference. The captain, unwilling to lose me, told a story altogether of his own framing: he gave me a very plausible account how he had missed a large

packet of letters and papers which he should
have brought with him; but this he said he was
sure of, having had it from my father's own
mouth, as well as from his employer, that a person lately dead had left me £400 a year; adding
further, that if I was any way embarrassed in my
circumstances he had express orders to redeem
me, though it should cost one half of his cargo.
Every particular of this was false; nor could I
myself believe what he said about the estate; but
as I had some expectation from an aged relative,
I thought a part of it might be true. But I was
not long in suspense; for though my father's care
and desire to see me had too little weight with
me, and would have been insufficient to make me
quit my retreat; yet the remembrance of Mrs.
N——, the hope of seeing her, and the possibility that accepting this offer might once more put
me in a way of gaining her hand, prevailed over
all other considerations. The captain further
promised (and in this he kept his word) that I
should lodge in his cabin, dine at his table, and
be his constant companion, without expecting
any service from me. And thus I was suddenly
freed from a captivity of about fifteen months.
I had neither a thought nor a desire of this change
one hour before it took place. I embarked with
him, and in a few hours lost sight of Kittam.

How much is their blindness to be pitied who

can see nothing but chance in events of this sort! So blind and stupid was I at that time, I made no reflection, I sought no direction in what had happened: like a wave of the sea, driven with the wind and tossed, I was governed by present appearances, and looked no farther. But He who is eyes to the blind was leading me in a way that I knew not.

Now I am in some measure enlightened, I can easily perceive that it is in the adjustment and concurrence of these seemingly fortuitous cir-cumstances, that the ruling power and wisdom of God is most evidently displayed in human affairs. How many such casual events may we remark in the history of Joseph, which had each a necessary influence on his ensuing promotion! If he had not dreamed, or if he had not told his dream; if the Midianites had passed by a day sooner, or a day later; if they had sold him to any person but Potiphar; if his mistress had been a better woman; if Pharaoh's officers had not displeased their lord; or if any, or all these things had fallen out in any other manner or time than they did, all that followed had been prevented; the promises and purposes of God concerning Israel, their bondage, deliverance, polity and settlement, must have failed; and as all these things tended to, and centered in Christ, the promised Savior, the desire of all nations, would not have appeared. Mankind had been still in their sins, without hope, and the counsels of God's eternal love in favor of sinners defeated. Thus we may see a connection between Joseph's first dream and the death of our Lord Jesus Christ, with all its glorious consequences. So strong, though secret, is the concatenation between the *greatest* and the *smallest* events. What a comfortable thought is this to a believer —to know that, amidst all the various interfering designs of men, the Lord has one constant design which he cannot, will not, miss ; namely, his own glory in the complete salvation of his people ; and that he is wise, and strong, and faithful, to make even those things which seem contrary to this design, subservient to promote it. You have allowed me to comment upon my own text ; yet the length of this observation may need some apology.

LETTER VII

Trading on the African coast.—Dangerous voyage for England

The ship I was now on board as a passenger, was on a trading voyage for gold, ivory, dyer's wood and bees-wax. It requires a long time to collect a cargo of this sort. The captain began his trade at Gambia, had been already four or five months in Africa, and continued there a year, or thereabouts, after I was with him; in which time we ranged the whole coast as far as Cape Lopez, which lies about a degree south of the equinoctial, and more than a thousand miles farther from England than the place where I embarked. I have little to offer worthy your notice in the course of this tedious voyage. I had no business to employ my thoughts, but sometimes amused myself with mathematics: excepting this, my life, when awake, was a course of most horrid impiety and profaneness. I know not that I have ever since met so daring a blasphemer: not content with common oaths and imprecations, I daily invented new ones; so that I was often seriously reproved by the captain, who was him-

self a very passionate man, and not at all circum-
spect in his expressions. From the relation I at
times made him of my past adventures, and what
he saw of my conduct, and especially toward the
close of the voyage, when he met with many
disasters, he would often tell me that, to his
grief, he had a Jonah on board; that a curse attended me wherever I went; and that all the
troubles he met with in the voyage were owing
to his having taken me into the vessel. I shall
omit any further particulars, and after mentioning an instance or two of the Lord's mercy to
me while I was thus defying his power and
patience, I shall proceed to something more
worthy your perusal.

Although I lived long in the excess of almost
every other extravagance, I never was fond of
drinking; and my father has often been heard to
say, that while I avoided drunkenness he should
still entertain hopes of my recovery. But sometimes I would promote a drinking-bout for the
sake of a frolic, as I termed it; for though I did
not love the liquor, I was sold to do iniquity,
and delighted in mischief. The last abominable
frolic of this sort I engaged in was in the river
Gabon: the proposal and expense were my own.
Four or five of us one evening sat down upon
deck to see who could hold out longest in drinking geneva and rum alternately: a large sea-

shell supplied the place of a glass. I was very unfit for a challenge of this sort; for my head was always incapable of bearing much strong drink. However, I began, and proposed the first toast, which I well remember was some imprecation against the person who should *start* first. This proved to be myself. My brain was soon fired. I arose and danced about the deck like a madman; and while I was thus diverting my companions my hat went overboard. By the light of the moon I saw the ship's boat, and eagerly threw myself over the side to get into her, that I might recover my hat. My sight in that circumstance deceived me; for the boat was not within my reach, as I thought, but perhaps twenty feet from the ship's side. I was, however, half overboard, and should in one moment more have plunged myself into the water, when somebody caught hold of my clothes behind, and pulled me back. This was an amazing escape; for I could not swim if I had been sober; the tide ran very strong; my companions were too much intoxicated to save me; and the rest of the ship's company were asleep. So near was I, to all appearance, of perishing in that dreadful condition, and sinking into eternity under the weight of my own curse!

Another time, at Cape Lopez, some of us had been in the woods and shot a buffalo, or wild cow; we brought a part of it on board, and care-fully marked the place (as I thought) where we left the remainder. In the evening we returned to fetch it; but we set out too late. I undertook to be the guide; but night coming on before we could reach the place, we lost our way. Some-times we were in swamps, up to the middle in wa-ter; and when we recovered dry land, we could not tell whether we were walking toward the ship, or wandering farther from her. Every step increased our uncertainty. The night grew dark-er, and we were entangled in inextricable woods, where, perhaps, the foot of man had never trod before. That part of the country is entirely aban-doned to wild beasts, with which it prodigiously abounds. We were, indeed, in a terrible case; having neither light, food nor arms, and expect-ing a tiger to rush from behind every tree. The stars were clouded, and we had no compass to form a judgment which way we were going. Had things continued thus, we had probably perished; but as it pleased God, no beast came near us; and after some hours' perplexity, the moon arose, and pointed out the eastern quarter. It appeared then, as we had expected, that, instead of draw-ing nearer to the sea-side, we had been penetrat-ing into the country; but by the guidance of the moon we at length came to the water-side, a con-siderable distance from the ship. We got safe on board without any other inconvenience than what we suffered from fear and fatigue.

These, and many other deliverances, were all at that time entirely lost upon me. The admonitions of conscience, which, from successive repulses had grown weaker and weaker, at length entirely ceased; and for a space of many months, if not for some years, I cannot recollect that I had a single check of that sort. At times I have been visited with sickness, and have believed myself near to death; but I had not the least concern about the consequences. In a word, I seemed to have every mark of final impenitence and rejection; neither judgments nor mercies made the least impression on me.

At length, our business finished, we left Cape Lopez, and after a few days' stay at the island of Annabona, to lay in provisions, we sailed homeward, about the beginning of January, 1748. From Annabona to England, without touching at any intermediate port, is a very long navigation, perhaps more than seven thousand miles, if we include the circuit necessary to be made on account of the trade-winds. We sailed first westward, till near the coast of Brazil, then northward, to the Banks of Newfoundland, with the usual variations of wind and weather, and without meeting any thing extraordinary. On these Banks we stopped half a day to fish for cod   this was then chiefly for diversion ; we had provisions enough, and little expected those fish (as it afterward proved) would be all we should have to subsist on. We left the Banks March 1, with a hard gale of wind westerly, which pushed us fast homeward. I should here observe that, with the length of this voyage in a hot climate, the vessel was greatly out of repair, and very unfit to support stormy weather ; the sails and cordage were likewise very much worn, and many such circumstances concurred to render what followed more dangerous. I think it was on the 9th of March, the day before our catastrophe, that I felt a thought pass through my mind which I had long been a stranger to. Among the few books we had on board, one was Stanhope's *Thomas à Kempis :* I carelessly took it up, as I had often done before, to pass away the time ; but I had still read it with the same indifference as if it was entirely a romance. However, while I was reading this time, an involuntary suggestion arose in my mind, What if these things should be true ? I could not bear the force of the inference, as it related to myself, and therefore shut the book presently. My conscience witnessed against me once more ; and I concluded that, true or false, I must abide the consequences of my own choice. I put an abrupt end to these reflections by joining in with some vain conversation or other that came in the way.

But now *the Lord's time was come*, and the conviction I was so unwilling to receive was deeply impressed upon me by an awful dispensation. I went to bed that night in my usual security and indifference, but was awakened from a sound sleep by the force of a violent sea which broke on board us. So much of it came down below as filled the cabin I lay in with water. This alarm was followed by a cry from the deck that the ship was going down, or sinking. As soon as I could recover myself I essayed to go upon deck; but was met upon the ladder by the captain, who desired me to bring a knife with me. While I returned for the knife another person went up in my room, who was instantly washed overboard. We had no leisure to lament him; nor did we expect to survive him long; for we soon found the ship was filling with water very fast. The sea had torn away the upper timbers on one side, and made the ship a mere wreck in a few minutes. I shall not affect to describe this disaster in the marine dialect, which would be understood by few; and therefore I can give you but a very inadequate idea of it. Taking in all circumstances, it was astonishing, and almost miraculous, that any of us survived to relate the story. We had immediately recourse to the pumps; but the water increased against all our efforts: some of us were set to *bailing* in another part of the vessel, that is, to lade it out with buckets and pails. We had but eleven or twelve people to sustain this service; and, notwithstanding all we could do, she was full, or very near it: and then, with a common cargo, she must have sunk of course; but we had a great quantity of beeswax and wood on board, which were specifically lighter than the water; and as it pleased God that we received this shock in the very crisis of the gale, toward morning we were enabled to employ some means for our safety, which succeeded beyond hope. In about an hour's time the day began to break, and the wind abated. We expended most of our clothes and bedding to stop the leaks; (though the weather was exceedingly cold, especially to us who had so lately left a hot climate;) over these we nailed pieces of boards, and at last perceived the water abate. At the beginning of this hurry I was little affected. I pumped hard, and endeavored to animate myself and my companions. I told one of them that in a few days this distress would serve us to talk of over a glass of wine: but he being a less hardened sinner than myself, replied with tears, "No, it is too late now." About nine o'clock, being almost spent with cold and labor, I went to speak with the captain, who was busied elsewhere; and just as I was returning from him, I said, almost without any meaning, "If this will not do, the Lord have mercy on us." This (though spoken with little reflection) was the first desire I had breathed for mercy for the space of many years. I was instantly struck with my own words, and as Jehu said once, *What hast thou to do with peace?* so it directly occurred, *What mercy can there be for me?* I was obliged to return to the pump, and there I continued till noon, almost every passing wave breaking over my head; but we made ourselves fast with ropes that we might not be washed away. Indeed, I expected that every time the vessel descended in the sea, she would rise no more; and though I dreaded death *now*, and my heart foreboded the worst, if the Scriptures, which I had long since opposed, were indeed true, yet still I was but half-convinced, and remained for a space of time in a sullen frame, a mixture of despair and impatience. I thought if the christian religion were true I could not be forgiven; and was therefore expecting, and almost, at times wishing, to know the worst of it.

LETTER VIII

Voyage for England continued.—His infidelity renounced

The 10th (that is, in the present style, the 21st) of March is a day much to be remembered by me; and I have never suffered it to pass wholly unnoticed since the year 1748: on that day the Lord sent from on high and delivered me out of deep waters. I continued at the pump from *three* in the *morning* till near *noon*, and then I could do no more. I went and lay down upon my bed, uncertain, and almost indifferent whether I should rise again. In an hour's time I was called; and not being able to pump, I went to the helm and steered the ship till midnight, excepting a short interval for refreshment. I had here leisure and convenient opportunity for reflection. I began to think of my former religious professions; the extraordinary turns in my life · the calls, warnings and deliverances I had met with; the licentious course of my conversation, particularly my unparalleled effrontery in making the gospel-history (which I could not then be sure was false, though I was not as yet assured it was true) the constant subject of profane ridicule. I thought, allowing the Scripture premises, there never was, nor could be, such a sinner as myself; and then, comparing the advantages I had broken through, I concluded, at first, that my sins were too great to be forgiven. The Scripture likewise seemed to say the same; for I had formerly been well acquainted with the Bible, and many passages, upon this occasion, returned upon my memory, particularly those awful passages, Prov. 1 : 24–31; Heb. 6 : 4–6; and 2 Pet 2 : 20, which seemed so exactly to suit my case and character as to bring with them a presumptive proof of a divine original. Thus, as I have said, I waited with fear and impatience to receive my inevitable doom. Yet though I had thoughts of this kind, they were exceedingly faint and disproportionate; it was not till long after, (perhaps several years,) till I had gained some clear views of the infinite righteousness and grace of Jesus Christ my Lord, that I had a deep and strong apprehension of my state by nature and practice: and perhaps till then I could not have borne the sight. So wonderfully does the Lord proportion the discoveries of sin and grace; for he knows our frame, and that if he were to put forth the greatness of his power, a poor sinner would be instantly overwhelmed, and crushed as a moth. But to return: when I saw, beyond all probability, there was still a hope of respite, and heard, about six in the evening, that the ship was freed from water, there arose a gleam of hope; I thought I saw the hand of God displayed in our favor: I began to pray. I could not utter the prayer of faith: I could not draw near to a reconciled God, and call him Father. My prayer was like the cry of the ravens, which yet the Lord does not disdain to hear. I now began to think of that Jesus whom I had so often derided; I recollected the particulars of his life, and of his death: a death for sins *not his own*, but, as I remembered, for the sake of those who in their distress should put their trust in him. And now I chiefly wanted evidence. The comfortless principles of infidelity were deeply riveted, and I rather wished than believed these things were real facts. You will please to observe, sir, that I collect the strain of the reasonings and exercises of my mind in one view; but I do not say that all this passed at one time. The great question now was, how to obtain *faith?* I speak not of an appropriating faith, (of which I then knew neither the nature nor necessity,) but how I should gain an assurance that the Scriptures were of divine inspiration, and a sufficient warrant for the exercise of trust and hope in God. One of the first helps I received (in consequence of a determination to examine the New Testament more carefully) was from Luke, 11 : 13. I had been sensible that to profess faith in Jesus

Christ, when in reality I did not believe his history, was no better than a mockery of the heart-searching God; but here I found a Spirit spoken of, which was to be communicated to those who ask it. Upon this I reasoned thus: If this book is true, the promise in this passage is true likewise: I have need of that very Spirit by which the whole was written, in order to understand it aright. He has engaged here to give that Spirit to those who ask. I must, therefore, pray for it; and if it is of God, he will make good his own word. My purposes were strengthened by John, 7 : 17. I concluded from thence, that though I could not say from my heart that I believed the Gospel, yet I would for the present take it for granted, and that by studying it in this light I should be more and more confirmed in it. If what I am writing could be perused by our modern infidels, they would say (for I too well know their manner) that I was very desirous to persuade myself into this opinion. I confess I was; and so would they be, if the Lord should show them, as he was pleased to show me at that time, the absolute necessity of some expedient to interpose between a righteous God and a sinful soul. Upon the Gospel-scheme I saw at least a peradventure of hope, but on every other side I was surrounded with black, unfathomable despair.

The wind was now moderate, but continued fair, and we were still drawing nearer to our port. We began to recover from our consternation, though we were greatly alarmed by our circumstances. We found that the water having floated all our moveables in the hold, all the casks of provision had been beaten to pieces by the violent motion of the ship; on the other hand, our live stock, such as pigs, sheep and poultry, had been washed overboard in the storm. In effect, all the provisions we saved, except the fish I mentioned, and some food of the pulse kind, which used to be given to the hogs, (and there was but little of this left,) all our other provisions would have subsisted us but a week at scanty allowance. The sails, too, were mostly blown away, so that we advanced but slowly even while the wind was fair. We imagined ourselves about a hundred leagues from the land, but were in reality much farther. Thus we proceeded with an alternate prevalence of hopes and fears. My leisure time was chiefly employed in reading and meditating on the Scripture, and praying to the Lord for mercy and instruction.

Things continued thus for four or five days, or perhaps longer, till we were awakened one morning by the joyful shouts of the watch upon deck proclaiming the sight of land. We were all soon raised at the sound. The dawning was uncommonly beautiful, and the light (just strong enough to discover distant objects) presented us with a gladdening prospect: it seemed a mountainous coast, about twenty miles from us, terminating in a cape or point; and a little further two or three small islands, or hummocks, as just rising out of the water; the appearance and position seemed exactly answerable to our hopes, resembling the north-west extremity of Ireland, which we were steering for. We sincerely congratulated each other, making no doubt but that, if the wind continued, we should be in safety and plenty the next day. We ate up the residue of our bread for joy at this welcome sight, and were in the condition of men suddenly reprieved from death. While we were thus alert, the mate, with a graver tone than the rest, sunk our spirits by saying " that he wished it might prove land at last." If one of the common sailors had first said so, I know not but the rest would have beat him for raising such an unreasonable doubt. It brought on, however, warm debates and disputes, whether it was land or not; but the case was soon unanswerably decided, for the day was advancing fast, and in a little time one of our fancied islands began to grow red from the approach of the sun, which soon arose just under it. In a word, we had been prodigal of our bread too hastily; our land was nothing but clouds;

and in half an hour more the whole appearance was dissipated. Seamen have often known deceptions of this sort, but in our extremity we were very loth to be undeceived. However, we comforted ourselves that though we could not see the land yet, we should soon, the wind hitherto continuing fair. But, alas! we were deprived of this hope likewise. That very day our fair wind subsided into a calm, and the next morning the gales sprung up from the southeast, directly against us, and continued so for more than a fortnight afterward. The ship was so wrecked that we were obliged to keep the wind always on the broken side, unless the weather was quite moderate. Thus we were driven, by the wind fixing in that quarter, still further from our port, to the northward of all Ireland, as far as the Lewis, or western islands of Scotland, but a long way to the westward. In a word, our station was such as deprived us of any hope of being relieved by other vessels. It may, indeed, be questioned whether our ship was not the very first that had been in that part of the ocean at the same season of the year.

Provisions now began to grow very short: the half of a salted cod was a day's subsistence for twelve people. We had plenty of fresh water, but no bread, hardly any clothes, and very cold weather. We had incessant labor with the pumps to keep the ship above water. Much labor and little food wasted us fast, and one man died under the hardship. Yet our sufferings were light in comparison to our just fears. We could not afford this bare allowance much longer, but had a terrible prospect of being either starved to death, or reduced to feed upon one another. Our expectations grew darker every day; and I had a further trouble, peculiar to myself. The captain, whose temper was quite soured by distress, was hourly reproaching me (as I formerly observed) as the sole cause of the calamity; and was confident that if I was thrown overboard, and not otherwise, they should be preserved from death. He did not intend to make the experiment; but the continual repetition of this in my ears gave me much uneasiness, especially as my conscience seconded his words; I thought it very probable that all that had befallen us was on my account. I was at last found out by the powerful hand of God, and condemned in my own breast. However, proceeding in the method I have described, I began to conceive hopes greater than all my fears; especially when, at the time we were ready to give up all for lost, and despair was taking place in every countenance, I saw the wind come about to the very point we wished it, so as best to suit that broken part of the ship which must be kept out of the water, and to blow so gentle as our few remaining sails could bear; and thus it continued, without any observable alteration or increase, though at an unsettled time of the year, till we once more were called up to see the land, and were convinced that it was land indeed. We saw the island Tory, and the next day anchored in Lough Swilly, in Ireland. This was the 8th of April, just four weeks after the damage we sustained from the sea. When we came into this port our very last victuals was boiling in the pot; and before we had been there two hours, the wind, which seemed to have been providentially restrained till we were in a place of safety, began to blow with great violence; so that, if we had continued at sea that night, in our shattered enfeebled condition, we must, in all human appearance, have gone to the bottom. About this time I began to know that there is a God that hears and answers prayer. How many times has he appeared for me since this great deliverance! yet, alas! how distrustful and ungrateful is my heart unto this hour.

LETTER IX

Voyage to England concluded—Apparent Conversion—1748

I have brought my history down to the time of my arrival in Ireland, 1748; but before I proceed I would look back a little to give you some further account of the state of my mind, and how far I was helped against inward difficulties, which beset me at the time I had many outward hardships to struggle with. The straits of hunger, cold, weariness, and the fears of sinking and starving, I shared in common with others: but besides these, I felt a heart-bitterness which was properly my own; no one on board but myself being impressed with any sense of the hand of God in our danger and deliverance, at least not awakened to any concern for their souls. No temporal dispensations can reach the heart unless the Lord himself applies them. My companions in danger were either quite unaffected, or soon forgot it all; but it was not so with me; not that I was any wiser or better than they, but because the Lord was pleased to vouchsafe me peculiar mercy; otherwise I was the most unlikely person in the ship to receive an impression, having been often before quite stupid and hardened in the very face of great dangers, and having always, till this time, hardened my neck still more and more after every reproof. I can see no reason why the Lord singled me out for mercy, but this, " that so it seemed good to him;" unless it was to show by one astonishing instance, that " with him nothing is impossible."

There were no persons on board to whom I could open myself with freedom concerning the state of my soul, none from whom I could ask advice. As to books, I had a New Testament, Stanhope, already mentioned, and a volume of Bishop Beveridge's Sermons, one of which, upon our Lord's Passion, affected me much. In perusing the New Testament, I was struck with several passages, particularly that of the fig-tree, Luke, 13; the case of St. Paul, 1 Tim. 1; but particularly the prodigal, Luke, 15; a case I thought had never been so nearly exemplified as by myself: and then the goodness of the father in receiving, nay, in running to meet such a son; and this intended only to illustrate the Lord's goodness to returning sinners: this gained upon me. I continued much in prayer; I saw that the Lord had interposed *so far* to save me; and I hoped he would do more. The outward circumstances helped in this place to make me still more serious and earnest in crying to Him who alone could relieve me; and sometimes I thought I could be content to die even for want of food, if I might but die a believer. Thus far I was answered, that before we arrived in Ireland I had a satisfactory evidence in my own mind of the truth of the Gospel, as considered in itself, and its exact suitableness to answer all my needs. I saw that by the way there pointed out, God might declare, not his mercy only, but his justice also, in the pardon of sin, on account of the obedience and sufferings of Jesus Christ. My judgment at that time embraced the sublime doctrine of " God manifest in the flesh, reconciling the world to himself." I had no idea of those systems which allow the Savior no higher honor than that of an *upper servant*, or, at the most, a *demi-god*. I stood in need of an almighty Savior, and such a one I found described in the New Testament. Thus far the Lord had wrought a marvellous thing; I was no longer an infidel; I heartily renounced my former profaneness; I had taken up some right notions, was seriously disposed, and sincerely touched with a sense of the undeserved mercy I had received, in being brought safe through so many dangers. I was sorry for my past misspent life, and purposed an immediate reformation: I was quite freed from the habit of swearing, which seemed to have been deeply rooted in me as a second nature. Thus, to all appearance, I was a new man.

But though I cannot doubt that this change, so far as it prevailed, was wrought by the Spirit and power of God; yet still I was greatly deficient in many respects. I was, in some degree, affected with a sense of my more enormous sins; but I was little aware of the innate evils of my heart. I had no apprehension of the spirituality and extent of the law of God; the hidden life of a christian, as it consists in communion with God by Jesus Christ; and a continual dependance on him for hourly supplies of wisdom, strength and. comfort, was a mystery of which I had as yet no knowledge. I acknowledged the Lord's mercy in pardoning what was past, but depended chiefly upon my own resolution to do better for the time to come. I had no christian friend or faithful minister to advise me that my strength was no more than my righteousness; and though I soon began to inquire for serious books, yet, not having spiritual discernment, I frequently made a wrong choice; and I was not brought in the way of evangelical preaching or conversation (except a few times when I heard but understood not) for six years after this period. Those things the Lord was pleased to discover to me gradually. I learned them here a little and there a little, by my own painful experience, at a distance from the common means and ordinances, and in the midst of the same course of evil company and bad examples as I had been conversant with for some time. From this period I could no more make a mock at sin, or jest with holy things; I no more questioned the truth of Scripture, or lost a sense of the rebukes of conscience. Therefore I consider this as the beginning of my return to God, or rather of his return to me; but I cannot consider myself to have been a believer (in the full sense of the word) till a considerable time afterward.

I have told you that, in the time of our distress, we had fresh water in abundance. This was a considerable relief to us, especially as our spare diet was mostly salt-fish, without bread; we drank plentifully, and were not afraid of wanting water; yet our stock of this likewise was much nearer to an end than we expected; we supposed that we had six large butts of water on board; and it was well that we were safe arrived in Ireland before we discovered that five of them were empty, having been removed out of their places, and stove by the violent agitation when the ship was full of water. If we had found this out while we were at sea, it would have greatly heightened our distress, as we must have drunk more sparingly.

While the ship was refitting at Lough Swilly, I repaired to Londonderry. I lodged at an exceedingly good house, where I was treated with much kindness, and soon recruited my health and strength. I was now a serious professor, went twice a-day to the prayers at church, and was, at times, very particular and earnest in my private devotion; but yet, for want of a better knowledge of myself, and the subtlety of Satan's temptations, I was soon seduced to forget the vows of God that were upon me. One day as I was abroad with the mayor of the city, and some other gentlemen, shooting, I climbed up a steep bank, and pulling my fowling-piece after me, as I held it in a perpendicular direction, it went off so near my face as to burn away the corner of my hat. Thus, when we think ourselves in the greatest safety, we are no less exposed to danger than when all the elements seem conspiring to destroy us. The Divine Providence, which is sufficient to deliver us in our utmost extremity, is equally necessary to our preservation in the most peaceful situation.

During our stay in Ireland I wrote home. The vessel I was in had not been heard of for eighteen months, and was given up for lost long before. My father had no more expectation of hearing that I was alive; but he received my letter a few days before he left London. He was just going governor of York Fort, in Hudson's Bay, from whence he never returned. He sailed before I landed in England, or he had purposed to take me with him; but God designing otherwise one hinderance or another delayed us in Ireland until it was too late. I received two or three affectionate letters from him, but I never had the pleasure of seeing him more. I had hopes that, in three years more, I should have had an opportunity of asking his forgiveness for the uneasiness my disobedience had given him; but the ship that was to have brought him home came without him. According to the best accounts we received, he was seized with the cramp when bathing, and drowned, a little before her arrival in the bay. Excuse this digression.

My father, willing to contribute all in his power to my satisfaction, paid a visit, before his departure, to my friends in Kent, and gave his consent to the union which had been so long talked of. Thus, when I returned to —— I found I had only the consent of one person to obtain; with her I as yet stood at as great an uncertainty as on the first day I saw her.

I arrived at Liverpool the latter end of May, 1748, about the same day that my father sailed from the Nore; but found the Lord had provided me another father in the gentleman whose ship had brought me home. He received me with great tenderness, and the strongest expressions of friendship and assistance; yet no more than he has since made good: for to him, as the instrument of God's goodness, I owe my all. Yet it

would not have been in the power even of this
friend to have served me effectually, if the Lord
had not met with me on my way home, as I have
related. Till then I was like the man possessed
with the *legion*. No arguments, no persuasion,
no views of interest, no remembrance of the past,
or regard to the future, could have constrained
me within the bounds of common prudence. But
now I was, in some measure, restored to my
senses. My friend immediately offered me the
command of a ship; but, upon mature consideration, I declined it for the present. I had been
hitherto always unsettled and careless; and
therefore thought I had better make another
voyage first, and learn to obey, and acquire a
further insight and experience in business before
I ventured to undertake such a charge. The mate
of the vessel I came home in was preferred to the
command of a new ship, and I engaged to go in
the station of mate with him. I made a short visit
to London, &c. which did not fully answer my
views. I had but one opportunity of seeing Mrs.
N ——, of which I availed myself very little; for
I was always exceedingly awkward in pleading
my own cause in our conversation. But after my
return to Liverpool I put the question in such a
manner, by letter, that she could not avoid (unless I had greatly mistaken her) coming to some
sort of an explanation. Her answer (though pen-

ned with abundance of caution) satisfied me ; as I collected from it that she was free from any other engagement, and not unwilling to wait the event of the voyage I had undertaken. I should be ashamed to trouble you with these little details, if you had not yourself desired me.

———

LETTER X

Sails for Africa as Mate —Sickness —Studies Latin

My connections with sea-affairs have often led me to think, that the varieties observable in christian experience may be properly illustrated from the circumstances of a voyage. Imagine to yourself a number of vessels, at different times, and from different places, bound to the same port ; there are some things in which all these would agree—the compass steered by, the port in view, the general rules of navigation, both as to the management of the vessel and determining their astronomical observations, would be the same in all. In other respects they would differ ; perhaps no two of them would meet with the same distribution of winds and weather. Some we see set out with a prosperous gale; and when they almost think their passage secured they are checked by adverse blasts; and, after enduring much hardship and danger, and frequent expectations of shipwreck, they just escape, and reach the desired haven. Others meet the greatest difficulties at first; they put forth in a storm, and are often beaten back; at length their voyage proves favorable, and they enter the port with a rich and abundant entrance. Some are hard beset with cruisers and enemies, and obliged to fight their way through; others meet with little remarkable in their passage. Is it not thus in the spiritual life? All true believers walk by the same rule, and mind the same things; the word of God is their compass; Jesus is both their polar star and their sun of righteousness; their hearts and faces are all set Zion-ward. Thus far they are as one body, animated by one spirit; yet their experience, formed upon these common principles, is far from being uniform. The Lord, in his first call, and his following dispensations, has a regard to the situation, temper and talents of each, and to the particular services or trials he has appointed them for. Though all are exercised at times, yet some pass through the voyage of life much more smoothly than others. But he " who walketh upon the wings of the wind, and measures the waters in the hollow of his hand," will not suffer any of whom he has once taken charge to perish in the storms, though for a season, perhaps, many of them are ready to give up all hopes.

We must not, therefore, make the experience of others, in all respects, a rule to ourselves, nor our own a rule to others; yet these are common mistakes, and productive of many more. As to myself, every part of my case has been extraordinary. I have hardly met a single instance resembling it. Few, very few, have been recovered from such a dreadful state; and the few that have been thus favored have generally passed through the most severe convictions; and after the Lord has given them peace, their future lives have been usually more zealous, bright, and exemplary than common. Now, as on the one hand my convictions were very moderate, and far below what might have been expected from the dreadful review I had to make; so, on the other, my first beginnings in a religious course were as faint as can be well imagined. I never knew that season alluded to, Jer. 2 : 2 ; Rev. 2 : 4, usually called *the time of the first love.* Who would not expect to hear that, after such a wonderful unhoped-for deliverance as I had received, and after my eyes were in some measure enlightened to see things aright, I should immediately cleave to the Lord and his ways with full purpose of heart, and consult no more with flesh and blood? But, alas! it was far otherwise with me. I had learned to pray; I set some value upon the word of God, and was no longer a libertine: but my soul still cleaved to the dust. Soon after my departure from Liverpool I began to intermit, and grow slack in waiting upon the Lord; I grew vain and trifling in my conversation; and though my heart smote me often, yet my armor was gone, and I declined fast; and by the time I arrived at Guinea I seemed to have forgot all the Lord's mercies, and my own engagements, and was (profaneness excepted) almost as bad as before. The enemy prepared a train of temptations, and I became his easy prey; and, for about a month, he lulled me asleep in a course of evil, of which, a few months before, I could not have supposed myself any longer capable. How much propriety is there in the apostle's advice, " Take heed, lest any of you be hardened through the deceitfulness of sin!" O, who can be sufficiently upon their guard! Sin first deceives, and then it hardens. I was now fast bound in chains; I had little desire, and no power at all, to recover myself. I could not but at times reflect how it was with me; but if I attempted to struggle with it, it was in vain. I was just like Samson when he said, "I will go forth and shake myself as at other times;" but the Lord was departed, and he found himself helpless in the hands of his enemies. By the remembrance of this interval, the Lord has often instructed me since, what a poor creature I am in myself, incapable of standing a single hour without continual fresh supplies of strength and grace from the fountain-head.

At length the Lord, whose mercies are infinite, interposed in my behalf. My business in this voyage, while upon the coast, was to sail from place to place in the long-boat, to purchase slaves The ship was at Sierra Leone, and I then at the Plantanes, the scene of my former captivity, where every thing I saw might remind me of my ingratitude. I was in easy circumstances, courted by those who formerly despised me : the *lime-trees* I had planted were growing tall, and promised fruit the following year ; against which time I had expectations of returning with a ship of my own. But none of these things affected me, till, as I have said, the Lord again interposed to save me. He visited me with a violent fever, which broke the fatal chain, and once more brought me to myself. But, O what a prospect ! I thought myself now summoned away. My past dangers and deliverances, my earnest prayers in the time of trouble, my solemn vows before the Lord, and my ungrateful returns for all his goodness, were all present to my mind at once. Then I began to wish that the Lord had suffered me to sink into the ocean when I first besought his mercy. For a little while I concluded the door of hope to be quite shut; but this continued not long. Weak, and almost delirious, I arose from my bed, and crept to a retired part of the island; and here I found a renewed liberty to pray. I durst make no more resolves, but cast myself before the Lord, to do with me as he should please. I do not remember that any particular text or remarkable discovery was presented to my mind; but, in general, I was enabled to hope and believe in a crucified Savior. The burden was removed from my conscience, and not only my peace but my health was restored; I cannot say instantaneously; but I recovered from that hour; and so fast, that when I returned to the ship, two days afterward, I was perfectly well before I got on board. And from that time, I trust, I have been delivered from the power and dominion of sin; though, as to the effects and conflicts of sin dwelling in me, I still "groan, being burdened." I now began again to wait upon the Lord; and though I have often grieved his Spirit, and foolishly wandered from him since, (when, alas, shall I be more wise!) yet his powerful grace has hitherto preserved me from such black declensions as this I have last recorded: and I humbly trust in his mercy and promises, that he will be my guide and guard to the end.

My leisure hours in this voyage were chiefly employed in learning the Latin language, which I had now entirely forgot. This desire took place from an imitation I had seen of one of Horace's odes in a magazine. I began the attempt under the greatest disadvantages possible ; for I pitch-ed upon a poet, perhaps the most difficult of the poets, even Horace himself, for my first book. I had picked up an old English translation of him, which, with Castalio's Latin Bible, were all my help. I forgot a dictionary, but I would not therefore give up my purpose. I had the edition *in usum Delphini ;* and, by comparing the odes with the interpretation, and tracing the words, I could understand from one place to another by the index, with the assistance I could get from the Latin Bible : in this way, by dint of hard in-dustry, often waking when I might have slept, I made some progress before I returned, and not only understood the sense and meaning of many odes, and some of the epistles, but began to re-lish the beauties of the composition, and acquired a spice of what Mr. Law calls *classical enthusiasm.* And indeed, by this means, I had Horace more in my mind than some who are masters of the Latin tongue ; for my helps were so few, that I generally had the passage fixed in my memory before I could fully understand its meaning.

My business in the long-boat, during the eight

months we were upon the coast, exposed me to innumerable dangers and perils, from burning suns and chilling dews, winds, rains and thunderstorms, in the open boat; and on shore, from long journeys through the woods, and the temper of the natives, who are in many places cruel, treacherous, and watching opportunities for mischief. Several boats in the same time were cut off, several white men poisoned, and in my own boat, I buried six or seven people with fevers. When going on shore, or returning from it, in their little canoes, I have been more than once or twice overset by the violence of the surf, or breach of the sea, and brought to land halfdead (for I could not swim.) An account of such escapes as I still remember, would swell to several sheets, and many more I have perhaps forgot : I shall only select one instance, as a specimen of that wonderful providence which watched over me for good, and which, I doubt not, you will think worthy of notice.

When our trade was finished, and we were near sailing to the West Indies, the only remaining service I had to perform in the boat was to assist in bringing the wood and water from the shore. We were then at Rio Cestors. I used to go into the river in the afternoon with the seabreeze, procure my loading in the evening, and return on board in the morning with the land wind. Several of these little voyages I had made; but the boat was become old and almost unfit for use. The service likewise was almost completed. One day, having dined on board, I was preparing to return to the river as formerly: I had taken leave of the captain, received his orders, was ready in the boat, and just going to put off, as we term it, that is, to let go our ropes and sail from the ship. In that instant the captain came up from the cabin, and called me on board again. I went, expecting further orders; but he said that he *took it in his head* (as he phrased it) that I should remain that day in the ship; and accordingly ordered another man to go in my room. I was surprised at this, as the boat had never been sent away without me before, and asked him the reason; he could give me no reason but as above, that so he would have it. Accordingly the boat went without me; but returned no more: she sunk that night in the river, and the person who had supplied my place was drowned. I was much struck when we received news of the event the next morning. The captain himself, though quite a stranger to religion, so far as to deny a particular providence, could not help being affected; but he declared that he had no other reason for countermanding me at that time, but that it came suddenly into his mind to detain me.

LETTER XI

Marriage —First Voyage to Africa as Captain —Study of Latin exchanged for the Scriptures

A few days after I was thus wonderfully saved from an unforeseen danger we sailed for Antigua, and from thence proceeded to Charleston, in South Carolina. In this place there are many serious people; but I knew not where to find them out: indeed I was not aware of a difference, but supposed that all who attended public worship were good christians. I was as much in the dark about preaching, not doubting but whatever came from the pulpit must be very good. I had two or three opportunities of hearing a dissenting minister, named Smith, who, by what I have known since, I believe to have been an excellent and powerful preacher of the Gospel; and there was something in his manner that struck me, but I did not rightly understand him. The best words that men can speak are ineffectual till explained and applied by the Spirit of God, who alone can open the heart. It pleased the Lord, for some time, that I should learn no more than what he enabled me to collect from my own experience and reflection. My conduct was now very incon sistent. Almost every day, when business would permit, I used to retire into the woods and fields (for these, when at hand, have always been my favorite oratories,) and I trust I began to taste the sweets of communion with God in the exercises of prayer and praise; and yet I frequently spent the evenings in vain and worthless company. Indeed my relish for worldly diversions was much weakened, and I was rather a spectator than a sharer in their pleasures; but I did not as yet see the necessity of an absolute forbearance. Yet as my compliance with custom and company was chiefly owing to want of light, rather than to an obstinate attachment, and the Lord was pleased to preserve me, in some good degree, I trust, from what I *knew* was sinful, I had, for the most part, peace of conscience, and my strongest desires were toward the things of God. As yet I knew not the force of that precept, "Abstain from all appearance of evil;" but very often ventured upon the brink of temptation; but the Lord was gracious to my weakness, and would not suffer the enemy to prevail against me. I did not break with the world at once, (as might, in my case, have been expected,) but I was gradually led to see the inconvenience and folly of one thing after another; and when I saw it, the Lord strengthened me to give it up. But it was some years before I was set quite at liberty from occasional compliances in many things, in which at this time I durst by no means allow myself.

We finished our voyage, and arrived in Liverpool. When the ship's affairs were settled, I went to London, and from thence (as you may suppose) I soon repaired to Kent. More than seven years had now elapsed since my first visit. No views of the kind could seem more chimerical, or could subsist under greater discouragements than mine had done; yet, through the overruling goodness of God, while I seemed abandoned to myself, and blindly following my own headstrong passions, I was guided by a hand that I knew not, to the accomplishment of my wishes. Every obstacle was now removed. I had renounced my former follies, my interest was established, and friends on all sides consenting, the point was now entirely between ourselves; and after what had passed, was easily concluded. Accordingly our hands were joined on the 1st of February, 1750.

The satisfaction I have found in this union, you will suppose has been greatly heightened by reflection on the former disagreeable contrasts I had passed through, and the views I have had of the singular mercy and providence of the Lord in bringing it to pass. If you please to look back to the beginning of my sixth letter, I doubt not but you will allow, that few persons have known more either of the misery or happiness of which human life (as considered in itself) is capable. How easily, at a time of life when I was so little capable of judging, (but a few months more than seventeen,) might my affections have been fixed where they could have met with no return, or where success would have been the heaviest disappointment. The long delay I met with was likewise a mercy; for had I succeeded a year or two sooner, before the Lord was pleased to change my heart, we must have been mutually unhappy, even as to the present life. "Surely mercy and goodness have followed me all my days!"

But, alas! I soon began to feel that my heart was still hard and ungrateful to the God of my life. This crowning mercy which raised me to all I could ask or wish in a temporal view, and which ought to have been an animating motive to obedience and praise, had a contrary effect. I rested in the gift, and forgot the Giver. My poor narrow heart was *satisfied*. A cold and careless frame, as to spiritual things, took place, and gained ground daily. Happily for me the season was advancing, and in June I received orders to repair to Liverpool. This roused me from my dream. I need not tell you that I found the pains of absence and separation fully proportioned to my preceding pleasure. It was hard, very hard to part, especially as conscience interfered, and suggested to me how little I deserved that we should be spared to meet again. But the Lord supported me. I was a poor, faint, idolatrous creature; but I had now some acquaintance with the way of access to a throne of grace by the blood of Jesus; and peace was soon restored to my conscience. Yet, through all the following voyage my irregular and excessive affections were as thorns in my eyes, and often made my other blessings tasteless and insipid. But He who doeth all things well over-ruled this likewise for good. It became an occasion of quickening me in prayer both for my wife and myself; it increased my indifference for company and amusement; it habituated me to a kind of voluntary self-denial, which I was afterward taught to improve to a better purpose.

While I remained in England we corresponded every post; and all the while I used the sea afterward, I constantly kept up the practice of writing two or three times a-week, (if weather and business permitted,) though no conveyance homeward offered for six or eight months together. My packets were usually heavy; and as not one of them at any time miscarried, I have to the amount of nearly two hundred sheets of paper now lying in my bureau of that correspondence. I mention this little relief by which I contrived to soften the intervals of absence, because it had a good effect beyond my first intention. It habituated me to think and write upon a great variety of subjects; and I acquired, insensibly, a greater readiness of expressing myself than I should otherwise have attained. As I gained more ground in religious knowledge, my letters became more serious ; and, at times, I still find an advantage in looking them over ; especially as they remind me of many providential incidents, and the state of my mind at different periods in these voyages, which would otherwise have escaped my memory.

I sailed from Liverpool in August, 1750, commander of a good ship. I have no very extraordinary events to recount from this period, and shall therefore contract my memoirs lest I become tedious: yet I am willing to give you a brief sketch of my history down to 1755, the year of my settlement in my present situation. I had now the command and care of thirty persons ; I endeavored to treat them with humanity, and to set them a good example : I likewise established public worship, twice every Lord's-day, officiating myself. Farther than this I did not proceed while I continued in that employment.

Having now much leisure, I prosecuted the study of the Latin with good success. I took a

dictionary this voyage, and procured two or
three other books; but still it was my hap to
choose the hardest. I added Juvenal to Horace;
and, for prose authors, I pitched upon Livy, Cæsar
and Sallust. You will easily conceive, sir, that I
had hard work to begin (where I should have left
off) with Horace and Livy. I was not aware of
the difference of style: I had heard Livy highly
commended, and I was resolved to understand
him. I began with the first page, and laid down
a rule, which I seldom departed from, not to proceed to a second period till I understood the first,
and so on. I was often at a stand, but seldom
discouraged: here and there I found a few lines
quite obstinate, and was forced to break in upon
my rule, and give them up, especially as my edition had only the text, without any notes to assist me. But there were not many such; for before the close of that voyage I could (with a few
exceptions) read Livy from end to end, almost
as readily as an English author. And I found, in
surmounting this difficulty, I had surmounted all
in one. Other prose authors, when they came in
my way, cost me little trouble. In short, in the
space of two or three voyages I became tolerably acquainted with the best classics; (I put all
I have to say upon this subject together;) I read
Terence, Virgil, and several pieces of Cicero, and
the modern classics, Buchanan, Erasmus and Cas-

simir. At length I conceived a design of becom-
ing a Ciceronian myself, and thought it would be
a fine thing indeed to write pure and elegant Latin. I made some essays toward it, but by this
time the Lord was pleased to draw me nearer to
himself, and to give me a fuller view of the
"pearl of great price," the inestimable treasure
hid in the field of the Holy Scriptures; and, for
the sake of this, I was made willing to part with
all my newly-acquired riches. I began to think
that life was too short (especially my life) to admit of leisure for such elaborate trifling. Neither
poet nor historian could tell me a word of Jesus,
and I therefore applied myself to those who could.
The classics were at first restrained to one morning in the week, and at length quite laid aside. I
have not looked into Livy these five years, and
I suppose I could not now well understand him.
Some passages in Horace and Virgil I still admire; but they seldom come in my way. I prefer Buchanan's Psalms to a whole shelf of Elze-
virs. But this much I have gained—and more
than this I am not solicitous about—so much of
the Latin as enables me to read any useful or
curious book that is published in that language.
About the same time, and for the same reason
that I quarrelled with Livy, I laid aside the mathematics. I found they not only cost me much
time, but engrossed my thoughts too far; my

head was literally full of *schemes*. I was weary of cold contemplative truths, which can neither warm nor amend the heart, but rather tend to aggrandize *self*. I found no traces of this wisdom in the life of Jesus or the writings of Paul I do not regret that I have had some opportunities of knowing the first principles of these things; but I see much cause to praise the Lord that he inclined me to stop in time; and, whilst I was "spending my labor for that which is not bread," was pleased to set before me "wine and milk, without money and without price."

My first voyage was fourteen months, through various scenes of danger and difficulty, but nothing very remarkable; and as I intend to be more particular with regard to the second, I shall only say that I was preserved from every harm; and having seen many fall on my right hand and on my left, I was brought home in peace, and restored to where my thoughts had been often directed, November 2, 1751.

LETTER XII

Second Voyage to Africa as Commander

I almost wish I could recall my last sheet, and retract my promise. I fear I have engaged too far, and shall prove a mere *egotist*. What have I more that can deserve your notice? However, it is some satisfaction that I am now writing to yourself only; and I believe you will have candor to excuse what nothing but a sense of your kindness could extort from me.

Soon after the period where my last closes, that is, in the interval between my first and second voyage after my marriage, I began to keep a sort of diary; a practice which I have since found of great use. I had in this interval repeated proofs of the ingratitude and evil of my heart. A life of ease in the midst of my friends, and the full satisfaction of my wishes, was not favorable to the progress of grace, and afforded cause of daily humiliation. Yet, upon the whole, I gained ground. I became acquainted with books which gave me a farther view of christian doctrine and experience; particularly, *Scougall's Life of God in the Soul of Man*, *Hervey's Medi-*

tations, and *the Life of Colonel Gardiner.* As to preaching, I heard none but the common sort, and had hardly an idea of any better; neither had I the advantage of christian acquaintance. I was likewise greatly hindered by a cowardly reserved spirit; I was afraid of being thought precise; and though I could not live without prayer, I durst not propose it even to my wife, till she herself first put me upon it: so far was I from those expressions of zeal and love which seem so suitable to the case of one who has had much forgiven. In a few months the returning season called me abroad again, and I sailed from Liverpool in a new ship, July, 1752.

A seafaring life is necessarily excluded from the benefit of public ordinances and christian communion; but, as I have observed, my loss upon these heads was at this time but small. In other respects, I know not any calling that seems more favorable, or affords greater advantages to an awakened mind, for promoting the life of God in the soul; especially to a person who has the command of a ship, and thereby has it in his power to restrain gross irregularities in others, and to dispose of his own time; and still more so in African voyages, as these ships carry a double proportion of men and officers to most others, which made my department very easy; and, excepting the hurry of trade, &c. upon the coast, which is rather occasional than constant, afforded me abundance of leisure. To be at sea in these circumstances, withdrawn out of the reach of innumerable temptations, with opportunity and turn of mind disposed to observe the wonders of God in the great deep; with the two noblest objects of sight, the expanded *heavens* and the expanded *ocean*, continually in view; and where evident interpositions of Divine Providence, in answer to prayer, occur almost every day; these are helps to quicken and confirm the life of faith, which, in a good measure, supply to a religious sailor the want of those advantages which can be enjoyed only upon the shore. And, indeed, though my knowledge of spiritual things, as knowledge is usually estimated, was at this time very small, yet I sometimes look back with regret upon these scenes. I never knew sweeter or more frequent hours of divine communion than in my last two voyages to Guinea, when I was either almost secluded from society on shipboard, or when on shore amongst the natives. I have wandered through the woods, reflecting on the singular goodness of the Lord to me, in a place where, perhaps, there was not a person that knew him for some thousand miles round me. Many a time, upon these occasions, I have restored the beautiful lines of Propertius to their right owner; lines full of blasphemy and madness when addressed to a creature, but full of comfort and propriety in the mouth of a believer.

Sic ego desertis possim bene vivere sylvis,
Quo nulla humano sit via trita pede :
Tu mihi curarum requies, in nocte vel atra
Lumen, et in solis tu mihi turba locis.

PARAPHRASED

In desert woods, with thee, my God,
Where human footsteps never trod,
   How happy could I be ;
Thou my repose from care, my light
Amidst the darkness of the night,
   In solitude my company.

In the course of this voyage I was wonderfully preserved in the midst of many obvious and many unforeseen dangers. At one time there was a conspiracy amongst my own people to turn pirates, and take the ship from me. When the plot was nearly ripe, and they waited only a convenient opportunity, two of those concerned in it were taken ill in one day; one of them died, and he was the only person I buried while on board. This suspended the affair, and opened a way to its discovery, or the consequence might have been fatal. The slaves on board were likewise frequently plotting insurrections, and were some-

times upon the very brink of mischief; but it
was always disclosed in due time. When I have
thought myself most secure, I have been sudden
ly alarmed with danger; and when I have almost
despaired of life, as sudden a deliverance has
been vouchsafed me. My stay upon the coast
was long, the trade very precarious; and, in pursuit of my business, both on board and on shore,
I was *in deaths oft*. Let the following instance
serve as a specimen:

I was at a place called *Mana*, near Cape Mount,
where I had transacted very large concerns; and
had, at the time I am speaking of, some debts
and accounts to settle which required my attendance on shore, and I intended to go the next morning. When I arose I left the ship, according to
my purpose, but when I came near the shore, the
surf, or breach of the sea ran so high that I was
almost afraid to attempt landing: indeed I had often ventured at a worse time; but I felt an inward
hinderance and backwardness, which I could
not account for: the surf furnished a pretext for
indulging it; and after waiting and hesitating for
about half an hour, I returned to the ship without
doing my business; which I think I never did
but that morning in all the time I used that trade.
But I soon perceived the reason of all this: It
seems, the day before I intended to land, a scan-
dalous and groundless charge had been laid

against me, (by whose instigation I could never learn,) which greatly threatened my honor and interest, both in Africa and England, and would perhaps, humanly speaking, have affected my life, if I had landed according to my intention. I shall, perhaps, enclose a letter which will give a full account of this strange adventure; and therefore shall say no more of it here, any further than to tell you that an attempt, aimed to destroy either my life or character, and which might, very probably, in its consequences, have ruined my voyage, passed off without the least inconvenience. The person most concerned owed me about a hundred pounds, which he sent me in a huff; and otherwise, perhaps, would not have paid me at all. I was very uneasy for a few hours, but was soon afterward comforted. I heard no more of my accusation till the next voyage; and then it was publicly acknowledged to be a malicious calumny, without the least shadow of a ground.

Such were the vicissitudes and difficulties through which the Lord preserved me. Now and then both faith and patience were sharply exercised; but suitable strength was given; and as such things did not occur every day, the study of the Latin, of which I gave a general account in my last, was renewed, and carried on from time to time when business would permit. I was mostly very regular in the management of my time; I allotted eight hours for sleep and meals, eight hours for exercise and devotion, and eight hours to my books: and thus, by diversifying my engagements, the whole day was agreeably filled up; and I seldom found a day too long, or an hour to spare. My studies kept me employed; and so far it was well; otherwise they were hardly worth the time they cost, as they led me to an admiration of false models and false maxims; an almost unavoidable consequence (I suppose) of an admiration of classic authors. Abating what I have attained of the language, I think I might have read *Cassandra* or *Cleopatra* to as good purpose as I read Livy, whom I now account an equal *romancer*, though in a different way.

From the coast I went to St. Christopher's, and here my idolatrous heart was its own punishment. The letters I expected from Mrs. Newton were by mistake forwarded to Antigua, which had been at first proposed as our port. As I was certain of her punctuality in writing, if alive, I concluded, by not hearing from her, that she was surely dead. This fear affected me more and more; I lost my appetite and rest; I felt an incessant pain in my stomach; and in about three weeks time I was near sinking under the weight of an imaginary stroke. I felt some severe symptoms of that mixture of pride and madness which is commonly called a *broken heart;* and indeed I wonder that this case is not more common than it appears to be. How often do the potsherds of the earth presume to contend with their Maker! and what a wonder of mercy is it that they are not all broken! However, my complaint was not all grief; conscience had a share. I thought my unfaithfulness to God had deprived me of her, especially my backwardness in speaking of spiritual things, which I could hardly attempt, even to her. It was this thought, that I had lost invaluable, irrecoverable opportunities, which both duty and affection should have engaged me to improve, that chiefly stung me; and I thought I would have given the world to know that she was living, that I might at least discharge my engagements by writing, though I was never to see her again. This was a sharp lesson; but I hope it did me good; and when I had thus suffered some weeks, I thought of sending a small vessel to Antigua. I did so; and she brought me several packets; which restored my health and peace, and gave me a strong contrast of the Lord's goodness to me, and my unbelief and ingratitude towards him.

In August, 1753, I returned to Liverpool My stay was very short at home that voyage—only six weeks. In that space nothing very memorable occurred; I shall therefore begin my next with an account of my third and last voyage. And thus I give both you and myself hopes of a speedy period to these memoirs, which begin to be tedious and minute even to myself; only I am animated by the thought that I write at your request; and have therefore an opportunity of showing myself   Yours, &c.

LETTER XIII

Third and last Voyage to Africa — Sickness — Religious experience

My third voyage was shorter and less perplexed than either of my former. Before I sailed I met with a young man who had formerly been a midshipman, and my intimate companion on board the Harwich. He was, at the time I first knew him, a sober youth; but I had found too much success in my unhappy attempts to infect him with libertine principles. When we met at Liverpool our acquaintance was renewed upon the ground of our former intimacy. He had good sense, and had read many good books. Our conversation frequently turned upon religion; and

I was very desirous to repair the mischief I had done him. I gave him a plain account of the manner and reason of my change, and used every argument to persuade him to relinquish his infidel schemes; and when I sometimes pressed him so close that he had no other reply to make, he would remind me that I was the very first person who had given him an idea of his liberty. This occasioned me many mournful reflections. He was then going master to Guinea himself; but before his ship was ready his merchant became a bankrupt, which disconcerted his voyage. As he had no farther expectations for that year, I offered to take him with me as a companion, that he might gain a knowledge of the coast; and the gentleman who employed me promised to provide for him upon his return. My view in this was not so much to serve him in his business, as to have an opportunity of debating the point with him at leisure; and I hoped, in the course of my voyage, my arguments, example and prayers, might have some good effect on him. My intention in this step was better than my judgment; and I had frequent reason to repent it. He was exceedingly profane, and grew worse and worse. I saw in him a most lively picture of what I had once been; but it was very inconvenient to have it always before my eyes. Besides, he was not only deaf to my remonstrances himself, but labored all he could to counteract my influence upon others. His spirit and passions were likewise exceedingly high; so that it required all my prudence and authority to hold him in any degree of restraint. He was as a sharp thorn in my side for some time; but at length I had an opportunity upon the coast of buying a small vessel, which I supplied with a cargo from my own, and gave him the command, and sent him away to trade on the ship's account. When we parted, I repeated and enforced my best advice. I believe his friendship and regard were as great as could be expected, when our principles were so diametrically opposite. He seemed greatly affected when I left him: but my words had no weight with him; when he found himself at liberty from under my eye, he gave a hasty loose to every appetite; and his violent irregularities, joined to the heat of the climate, soon threw him into a malignant fever, which carried him off in a few days. He died convinced, but not changed. The accounts I had from those who were with him were dreadful. His rage and despair struck them all with horror; and he pronounced his own fatal doom before he expired, without any appearance that he either *hoped* or *asked* for mercy. I thought this awful contrast might not be improper to give you, as a stronger view of the distinguishing goodness of God to me, the chief of sinners.

I left the coast in about four months, and sailed for St. Christopher's. Hitherto I had enjoyed a perfect state of health, equally in every climate, for several years; but upon this passage I was visited with a fever, which gave me a very near prospect of eternity. I have obtained liberty to enclose you three or four letters, which will more clearly illustrate the state and measure of my experience at different times than any thing I can say at present. One of them, you will find, was written at this period, when I could hardly hold a pen, and had some reason to believe I should write no more. I had not that "full assurance" which is so desirable at a time when flesh and heart fail; but my hopes were greater than my fears; and I felt a silent composure of spirit, which enabled me to wait the event without much anxiety. My trust, though weak in degree, was alone fixed upon the blood and righteousness of Jesus; and those words, "He is able to save to the uttermost," gave me great relief. I was for a while troubled with a very singular thought; whether it was a temptation, or that the fever disordered my faculties, I cannot say; but I seemed not so much afraid of wrath and punishment, as of being lost and overlooked amidst the myriads that are continually entering the unseen world. What is my soul, thought I, amongst such an innumerable multitude of beings? and this troubled me greatly. Perhaps the Lord will take no notice of me. I was perplexed thus for some time; but at last a text of Scripture, very apposite to the case, occurred to my mind, and put an end to the doubt: " The Lord knoweth them that are his." In about ten days, beyond the hope of those about me, I began to amend; and by the time of our arrival in the West Indies I was perfectly recovered. I hope this visitation was made useful to me.

Thus far, that is, for about the space of six years, the Lord was pleased to lead me in a secret way. I had learned something of the evil of my heart; I had read the Bible over and over, with several good books, and had a general view of *Gospel-truths;* but my conceptions were, in many respects, confused, not having in all this time met with one acquaintance who could assist my inquiries. But upon my arrival at St. Christopher's, on this voyage, I found a captain of a ship from London, whose conversation was greatly helpful to me. He was and is a member of Mr. Brewer's church, a man of experience in the things of God, and of a lively communicative turn. We discovered each other by some casual expressions in mixed company, and soon became, so far as business would permit, inseparable. For nearly a month we spent every evening together on board each other's ship alternately, and often prolonged our visits till toward day-break. I was all ear; and, what was better, he not only informed my understanding, but his discourse inflamed my heart. He encouraged me to open my mouth in social prayer; he taught me the advantage of christian converse; he put me upon an attempt to make my profession more public, and to venture to speak for God. From him, or rather from the Lord by his means, I received an increase of knowledge: my conceptions became clearer and more evangelical; and I was delivered from a fear which had long troubled me—the fear of relapsing into my former apostacy. But now I began to understand the security of the covenant of grace, and to expect to be preserved, not by my own power and holiness, but by the mighty power and promise of God, through faith in an unchangeable Savior. He likewise gave me a general view of the state of religion, with the errors and controversies of the times, (things to which I had been entirely a stranger,) and finally directed me where to apply in London for further instruction. With these newly-acquired advantages, I left him, and my passage homeward gave me leisure to digest what I had received. I had much comfort and freedom during those seven weeks, and my sun was seldom clouded. I arrived safely in Liverpool, August, 1754.

My stay at home was intended to be but short; and by the beginning of November I was again ready for the sea; but the Lord saw fit to over-rule my design. During the time I was engaged in the slave-trade I never had the least scruple as to its lawfulness. I was, upon the whole, satisfied with it, as the appointment Providence had marked out for me; yet it was, in many respects, far from eligible. It was, indeed, accounted a genteel employment, and usually very profitable, though to me it did not prove so, the Lord seeing that a large increase of wealth would not be good for me. However, I considered myself as a sort of *jailer* or *turnkey*, and I was sometimes shocked with an employment that was perpetually conversant with chains, bolts and shackles. In this view I had often petitioned, in my prayers, that the Lord, in his own time, would be pleased to fix me in a more humane calling, and, if it might be, place me where I might have more frequent converse with his people and ordinances, and be freed from those long separations from home, which very often were hard to bear. My prayers were now answered, though in a way I little expected. I now experienced another sudden, unforeseen change of life. I was within two days of sailing, and, to all appearance, in as good health as usual; but in the afternoon, as I was sitting with Mrs. Newton, drinking tea by ourselves, and talking over past events, I was in a moment seized with a fit which deprived me of sense and motion, and left me no other sign of life than that of breathing. I suppose it was of the apoplectic kind. It lasted about an hour; and when I recovered, it left a pain and dizziness in my head, which continued, with such symptoms as induced the physicians to judge it would not be safe or prudent for me to proceed on the voyage. Accordingly, by the advice of my friend to whom the ship belonged, I resigned the command the day before she sailed; and thus I was unexpectedly called from that service, and freed from a share of the future consequences of that voyage, which proved extremely calamitous. The person who went in my room, most of the officers, and many of the crew died, and the vessel was brought home with great difficulty.

As I was now disengaged from business, I left Liverpool, and spent most of the following year at London and in Kent. But I entered upon a new trial. You will easily conceive that Mrs. Newton was not an unconcerned spectator when I lay extended, and, as she thought, expiring, upon the ground. In effect, the blow that struck me reached her in the same instant: she did not indeed immediately feel it, till her apprehensions on my account began to subside; but as I grew better, she became worse: her surprise threw her into a disorder which no physicians could define, or medicines remove. Without any of the ordinary symptoms of a consumption, she decay.ed almost visibly, till she became so weak that she could hardly bear any one to walk across the room she was in. I was placed, for about eleven months, in what Dr. Young calls the

> ———dreadful post of observation,
> Darker every hour.

It was not till after my settlement at Liverpool that the Lord was pleased to restore her by his own hand, when all hopes from ordinary means were at an end. But before this took place I have some other particulars to mention, which must be the subject of the following sheet, which I hope will be the last on this subject from, &c.

LETTER XIV

Sickness of Mrs. Newton —Rural devotions —Residence in Liverpool —Studies Greek and Hebrew —Is refused ordination

By the directions I had received from my friend at St. Kitts, I soon found out a religious acquaintance in London. I first applied to Mr. Brewer, and chiefly attended upon his ministry when in town. From him I received many helps, both in public and private; for he was pleased to favor me with his friendship from the first. His kindness and the intimacy between us has continued and increased to this day; and of all my many friends, I am most deeply indebted to him. The late Mr. H——d was my second acquaintance, a man of a choice spirit, and an abundant zeal for the Lord's service. I enjoyed his correspondence till near the time of his death. Soon after, upon Mr. Whitefield's return from America, my two good friends introduced me to him; and though I had little personal acquaintance with him till afterward, his ministry was exceedingly useful to me. I had likewise access to some religious societies, and became known to many excellent christians in private life. Thus, when at London, I lived at the fountain-head, as it were, for spiritual advantages. When I was in Kent it was very different; yet I found some serious persons there; but the fine variegated woodland country afforded me advantages of another kind. Most of my time, at least some hours every day, I passed in retirement, when the weather was fair; sometimes in the thickest woods, sometimes on the highest hills, where almost every step varied the prospect. It has been my custom, for many years, to perform my devotional exercises *sub die*, when I have opportunity; and I always find these rural scenes have some tendency both to refresh and to compose my spirits. A beautiful diversified prospect gladdens my heart. When I am withdrawn from the noise and petty works of men, I consider myself as in the great temple which the Lord has built for his own honor.

The country between Rochester and Maidstone, bordering upon the Medway, was well suited to the turn of my mind; and were I to go over it now, I could point to many a place where I remember to have either earnestly sought, or happily found, the Lord's comfortable presence with my soul. And thus I lived, sometimes at London, and sometimes in the country, till the autumn of the following year. All this while I had two trials more or less upon my mind: the first and principal was Mrs. Newton's illness; she still grew worse, and I had daily more reason to fear that the hour of separation was at hand. When faith was in exercise, I was in some measure resigned to the Lord's will; but too often my heart rebelled, and I found it hard either to trust or to submit. I had likewise some care about my future settlement; the African trade was overdone that year, and my friends did not care to fit out another ship till mine returned. I was some time in suspense; but indeed a provision of food and raiment has seldom been a cause of great solicitude to me. I found it easier to trust the Lord in this point than in the former; and accordingly this was first answered. In August I received notice that I was nominated to the office of tide-surveyor. These places are usually obtained, or at least sought, by dint of much interest and application; but this came to me unsought and unexpected. I knew, indeed, my good friends in Liverpool had endeavored to procure another post for me, but found it pre-engaged. I found, afterward, that the place I had missed would have been very unsuitable for me; and that this, which I had no thought of, was the very thing I could have wished for, as it afforded me much leisure and the liberty of living in my own way. Several circumstances, unnoticed by others, concurred to show me that the good hand of the Lord was as remarkably concerned in this event, as in any other leading turn of my life.

But when I gained this point, my distress in the other was doubled; I was obliged to leave Mrs. Newton in the greatest extremity of pain and illness, when the physicians could do no more, and I had no ground of hope that I should see her again alive, but this—that nothing is impossible with the Lord. I had a severe conflict; but faith prevailed: I found the promise remarkably fulfilled, of strength proportioned to my need. The day before I set out, and not till then, the burden was entirely taken from my mind; I was strengthened to resign both her and myself to the Lord's disposal, and departed from her in a cheerful frame. Soon after I was gone she began to amend, and recovered so fast, that in about two months I had the pleasure to meet her at Stone, on her journey to Liverpool.

And now I think I have answered, if not exceeded your desire. Since October, 1755, we have been comfortably settled at Liverpool: and all my circumstances have been as remarkably smooth and uniform, as they were various in former years. My trials have been light and few; not but that I still find, in the experience of every day, the necessity of a life of faith. My principal trial is, the body of sin and death, which

makes me often to sigh out the apostle's complaint: "O wretched man!" but with him likewise I can say, "I thank God, through Jesus
Christ my Lord." I live in a barren land, where
the knowledge and power of the Gospel is very
low; yet here are a few of the Lord's people;
and this wilderness has been a useful school to
me, where I have studied more leisurely the
truths I gathered up in London. I brought down
with me a considerable stock of notional truth;
but I have since found that there is no effectual
teacher but God; that we can receive no farther
than he is pleased to communicate; and that no
knowledge is truly useful to me but what is made
my own by experience. Many things I thought
I had learned, would not stand in an hour of
temptation, till I had in this way learned them
over again. Since the year 1757 I have had an
increasing acquaintance in the West-riding of
Yorkshire, where the Gospel flourishes greatly.
This has been a good school to me: I have con-
versed at large among all parties, without joining
any; and in my attempts to hit the *golden mean*,
I have sometimes been drawn too near the different extremes; yet the Lord has enabled me to
profit by my mistakes. In brief, I am still a
learner, and the Lord still condescends to teach
me. I begin at length to see that I have attained but very little; but I trust in him to carry

on his own work in my soul, and, by all the dispensations of his grace and providence, to increase my knowledge of him and of myself.

When I was fixed in a house, and found my business would afford me much leisure time, I considered in what manner I should improve it. And now, having reason to close with the apostle's determination, " to know nothing but Jesus Christ and him crucified," I devoted my life to the prosecution of spiritual knowledge, and resolved to pursue nothing but in subservience to this main design. This resolution divorced me (as I have already hinted) from the classics and mathematics. My first attempt was to learn so much Greek as would enable me to understand the New Testament and Septuagint: and when I had made some progress this way, I entered upon the Hebrew the following year; and two years afterward, having surmised some advantages from the Syriac version, I began with that language. You must not think that I have attained, or ever aimed at, a critical skill in any of these: I had no business with them, but as in reference to something else. I never read one classic author in the Greek; I thought it too late in life to take such a round in this language as I had done in the Latin. I only wanted the signification of scriptural words and phrases; and for this I thought I might avail myself of *Scapula*, the *Synopsis*, and others, who had sustained the drudgery before me. In the Hebrew I can read the historical books and psalms with tolerable ease; but in the prophetical and difficult parts I am frequently obliged to have recourse to *lexicons*, &c. However, I know so much as to be able, with such helps as are at hand, to judge for myself the meaning of any passage I have occasion to consult. Beyond this I do not think of proceeding, if I can find better employment; for I would rather be some way useful to others, than die with the reputation of an eminent linguist.

Together with these studies I have kept up a course of reading of the best writers in divinity that have come to my hand, in the Latin and English tongues, and some French (for I picked up the French at times while I used the sea.) But within these two or three years I have accustomed myself chiefly to writing, and have not found time to read many books beside the Scriptures.

I am the more particular in this account, as my case has been something singular; for in all my literary attempts I have been obliged to strike out my own path, by the light I could acquire from books, as I have not had a teacher or assistant since I was ten years of age.

One word concerning my views to the *ministry*, and I have done. I have told you that this was my dear mother's hope concerning me; but her death, and the scenes of life in which I afterward engaged, seemed to cut off the probability. The first desires of this sort in my own mind arose many years ago, from a reflection on Gal. 1 : 23, 24, "But they had heard only, that he which persecuted us in times past, now preached the faith which once he destroyed. And they glorified God in me." I could not but wish for such a public opportunity to testify the riches of divine grace. I thought I was, above most living, a fit person to proclaim that faithful saying, "That Jesus Christ came into the world to save the chief of sinners;" and as my life had been full of remarkable turns, and I seemed selected to show what the Lord could do, I was in some hopes that perhaps, sooner or later, he might call me into his service.

I believe it was a distant hope of this that determined me to study the original Scriptures; but it remained an imperfect desire in my own breast, till it was recommended to me by some christian friends. I started at the thought when first seriously proposed to me; but afterward set apart some weeks to consider the case, to consult my friends, and to entreat the Lord's direction. The judgment of my friends, and many things that occurred, tended to engage me. My first thought was to join the Dissenters, from a presumption that I could not honestly make the required subscriptions: but Mr. C——, in a conversation upon these points, moderated my scruples; and preferring the Established Church in some other respects, I accepted a title from him some months afterward, and solicited ordination from the late Archbishop of York. I need not tell you I met a refusal, nor what steps I took afterward to succeed elsewhere. At present (1763) I desist from my applications. My desire to serve the Lord is not weakened; but I am not so hasty to push myself forward as I was formerly. It is sufficient that he knows how to dispose of me, and that he both can and will do what is best. To him I commend myself; I trust that his will and my true interest are inseparable. To his name be glory for ever. And thus I conclude my story, and presume you will acknowledge I have been particular enough.

CONTINUATION OF THE MEMOIR

BY REV. RICHARD CECIL

*Employment at Liverpool —Ministerial Labors at Olney six-
teen years —Acquaintance with J. Thornton, Esq. the poet
Cowper and Dr. Scott —Publications at Olney —Removal
to St. Mary Woolnoth, London,* 1779 *—Acquaintance with
Dr. Buchanan —Death of Mrs. Newton —Fruitfulness in
old age —Death*

Mr. Manesty, who had long been a faithful and
generous friend of Mr. Newton, procured him
the place of tide-surveyor in the port of Liverpool. Mr. Newton gives the following account
of it :—"I entered upon business yesterday. I
find my duty is to attend the tides one week, and
visit the ships that arrive, and such as are in the
river ; and the other week to inspect the vessels
in the docks ; and thus alternately the year round.
The latter is little more than a sinecure, but the
former requires pretty constant attendance, both
by day and night. I have a good office, with fire
and candle, and fifty or sixty people under my
direction ; with a handsome six-oared boat and a
cockswain to row me about in form." Letters to
a Wife, vol. 2. p. 7.

We cannot wonder that Mr. Newton latterly
retained a strong impression of a particular pro-

vidence superintending and conducting the steps of man, since he was so often reminded of it in his own history. The following occurrence is one of many instances: Mr. Newton, after his reformation, was remarkable for his punctuality; I remember his often sitting with his watch in his hand, lest he should fail in keeping his next engagement. This exactness with respect to time, it seems, was his habit while occupying his post at Liverpool. One day, however, some business had so detained him that he came to his boat much later than usual, to the surprise of those who had observed his former punctuality. He went out in the boat as heretofore to inspect a ship, but the ship blew up just before he reached her; it appears, that if he had left the shore a few minutes sooner, he must have perished with the rest on board.

This anecdote I had from a clergyman, upon whose word I can depend, who had been long on intimate terms with Mr. Newton, and who had it from Mr. Newton himself; the reason of its not appearing in his letters from Liverpool to Mrs. Newton, I can only suppose to be, his fearing to alarm her with respect to the dangers of his station. But another providential occurrence, which he mentions in those letters, I shall transcribe.

" When I think of my settlement here, and the manner of it, I see the appointment of Providence

so good and gracious, and such a plain answer
to my poor prayers, that I cannot but wonder and
adore. I think I have not yet told you, that my
immediate predecessor in office, Mr. C——, had
not the least intention of resigning his place on
the occasion of his father's death; though such
a report was spread about the town without his
knowledge, or rather in defiance of all he could
say to contradict it. Yet to this false report I
owe my situation. For it put Mr. M—— upon an
application to Mr. S——, the member for the
town; and the very day he received the promise in my favor, Mr. C—— was found dead in his
bed, though he had been in company, and in perfect health the night before. If I mistake not,
the same messenger who brought the promise
carried back the news of the vacancy to Mr.
S——, at Chester. About an hour after, the may-
or applied for a nephew of his; but, though it
was only an hour or two, he was too late. Mr.
S—— had already written, and sent off the letter,
and I was appointed accordingly. These circumstances appear to me extraordinary, though of a
piece with many other parts of my singular history. And the more so, as by another mistake I
missed the land-waiter's place, which was my
first object, and which I now see would not have
suited us nearly so well. I thank God I can now
look through instruments and second causes, and

see his wisdom and goodness immediately concerned in fixing my lot."

Mr. Newton having expressed, near the end of his narrative, the motives which induced him to aim at a regular appointment to the ministry in the Church of England, and the refusal he met with in his first making the attempt, the reader is farther informed that, on Dec. 16, 1758, Mr. Newton received a title to a curacy from the Rev. Mr. C——, and applied to the Archbishop of York, Dr. Gilbert, for ordination. The Bishop of Chester having countersigned his testimonials, directed him to Dr. Newton, the archbishop's chaplain. He was referred to the secretary, and received the softest refusal imaginable. The secretary informed him that he had " represented the matter to the archbishop, but his Grace was inflexible in supporting the rules and canons of the Church," &c

Travelling to Loughborough, Mr. Newton stopped at Welwyn, and sending a note to the celebrated Dr. Young, he received for answer, that the doctor would be glad to see him. He found the doctor's conversation agreeable, and to answer his expectation respecting the author of the Night Thoughts. The doctor likewise seemed pleased with Mr. Newton. He approved Mr. Newton's design of entering the ministry, and said many encouraging things upon the subject; and when he dismissed Mr. Newton, desired him never to pass near Welwyn without calling upon him.

Mr. Newton, it seems, had made some small attempts at Liverpool, in a way of preaching or expounding. Many wished him to engage more at large in those ministerial employments, to which his own mind was inclined; and he thus expresses his motives in a letter to Mrs. Newton, in answer to the objections she had formed. "The death of the late Rev. Mr. Jones, of St. Savior's, has pressed this concern more closely upon my mind. I fear it must be wrong, after having so solemnly devoted myself to the Lord for his service, to wear away my time, and bury my talents in silence, (because I have been refused orders in the Established Church,) after all the great things he has done for me."

In a note annexed, he observes, that "the influence of his judicious and affectionate counsellor moderated the zeal which dictated this letter, written in the year 1762; that had it not been for her, he should probably have been precluded from those important scenes of service to which he was afterward appointed:" but, he adds, "The exercises of my mind upon this point, I believe, have not been peculiar to myself. I have known several persons, sensible, pious, of competent abilities, and cordially attached to the established church; who, being wearied out with repeated refusals of ordination, and, perhaps, not having the advantage of such an adviser as I had, have at length struck into the itinerant path, or settled among the dissenters. Some of these, yet living, are men of respectable characters, and useful in their ministry."

In the year 1764 Mr. Newton had the curacy of Olney proposed to him, and was recommended by Lord Dartmouth to Dr. Green, bishop of Lincoln; of whose candor and tenderness he speaks with much respect. The bishop admitted him as a candidate for orders. "The examination," says he, "lasted about an hour, chiefly upon the principal heads of divinity. As I resolved not to be charged hereafter with dissimulation, I was constrained to differ from his lordship in some points; but he was not offended: he declared himself satisfied, and has promised to ordain me either next Sunday, in town, or the Sunday following, at Buckden. Let us praise the Lord."

Mr. Newton was ordained deacon at Buckden, April 29, 1764, and priest in June, the following year. In the parish of Olney he found many who not only had evangelical views of the truth, but had long walked in the light and experience of it. The vicarage was in the gift of the Earl of Dartmouth, the nobleman to whom Mr. Newton addressed the first twenty-six letters in his Car diphonia. The earl was a man of real piety and most amiable disposition; he had formerly appointed the Rev. Moses Brown, vicar of Olney. Mr. Brown was an evangelical minister, and a good man; he had afforded wholesome instruction to the parishioners of Olney, and had been the instrument of a sound conversion in many of them. He was the author of a poem, entitled Sunday Thoughts; a translation of Professor Zimmermann's Excellency of the Knowledge of Jesus Christ, &c.

But Mr. Brown had a numerous family, and met with considerable trials in it; he too much resembled Eli in his indulgence of his children. He was also under the pressure of pecuniary difficulties, and had therefore accepted the chaplaincy of Morden College, Blackheath, while vicar of Olney. Mr. Newton, in these circumstances, undertook the curacy of Olney, in which he continued nearly sixteen years, previous to his removal to St. Mary Woolnoth, to which he was afterward presented by the late John Thornton, Esq.

Mr. Newton was under the greatest obligations to Mr. Thornton's friendship while at Olney, and was enabled to extend his own usefulness by the bounty of that extraordinary man.

It is said of Solomon, that *the Lord gave him largeness of heart, even as the sand on the sea shore:* such a peculiar disposition for whatever was good or benevolent was also bestowed on

Mr. Thornton. He differed as much from rich men of ordinary bounty, as they do from others who are parsimonious. Nor was this bounty the result of occasional impulse, like a summer shower, violent and short: on the contrary, it proceeded like a river, pouring its waters through various countries, copious and inexhaustible. Nor could those obstructions of imposture and ingratitude, which have often been advanced as the cause of damming up other streams, prevent or·retard the course of this. The generosity of Mr. Thornton, indeed, frequently met with such hinderances, and led him to increasing discrimination; but the stream of his bounty never ceased to hold its course. Deep, silent and overwhelming, it still rolled on, nor ended even with his life.

But the fountain from whence this beneficence flowed, and by which its permanency and direction were maintained, must not be concealed. Mr. Thornton was a christian. Let no one, however, so mistake me here, as to suppose that I mean nothing more by the term CHRISTIAN, than the state of one, who convinced of the truth of Revelation, gives assent to its doctrines—regularly attends its ordinances—and maintains, externally, a moral and religious deportment. Such a one may have *a name to live while he is dead:* he may have *a form of godliness without the power* of it—he may even be found denying and ridi-

culing that power—till, at length, he can only be
convinced of his error at an infallible tribunal;
where a *widow*, who gives but a mite, or a *publi-
can*, who smites on his breast, shall be preferred
before him.

Mr. Thornton was a christian indeed; that is,
he was alive to God by a spiritual regeneration.
With this God he was daily and earnestly transacting that infinitely momentous affair, the salvation of his own soul; and, next to that, the salvation of the souls of others. Temperate in all
things, though mean in nothing, he made provision for doing good with his opulence : and seemed to be most in his element when appropriating
a considerable part of his large income to the ne-
cessities of others.

But Mr. Thornton possessed that discrimination in his attempts to serve his fellow-creatures,
which distinguishes an enlightened mind. He
habitually contemplated man, as one who has not
only a *body*, subject to want, affliction and death;
but a *spirit* also, which is immortal, and must be
happy or miserable for ever. He felt, therefore
that the noblest exertions of charity are those
which are directed to the relief of the noblest
part of our frame. Accordingly he left no mode
of exertion untried to relieve man under his natural ignorance and depravity. To this end, he
purchased advowsons and presentations, with a

view to place in parishes the most enlightened, active and useful ministers. He employed the extensive commerce in which he was engaged, as a powerful instrument for conveying immense quantities of Bibles, prayer-books, and other most useful publications, to every place visited by our trade. He printed at his own sole expense, large editions of the latter for that purpose; and it may safely be affirmed, that there is scarcely a part of the known world, where such books could be introduced, which did not feel the salutary influence of this single individual. Nor was Mr. Thornton limited in his views of promoting the interests of real religion, with what sect soever it was connected. He stood ready to assist a beneficial design in every party, but would be the creature of none. General good was his object: and, wherever or however it made its way, his maxim seemed constantly to be, *Valeat quantum valere potest.**

But the nature and extent of his liberality will be greatly misconceived, if any one should suppose it *confined* to moral and religious objects, though here were the grandest and most comprehensive exertions of it. Mr. Thornton was a philanthropist on the largest scale—the friend of man, under all his wants. His manner of relieving his fellow-men was princely. Instances might

* Be it as useful as possible.

be mentioned of it, were it proper to particularize, which would surprise those who did not
know Mr. Thornton. They were so much out of
ordinary course and expectation, that I know
some, who felt it their duty to inquire of him,
whether the sum they had received was sent by
his intention or by mistake. To this may be added, that the manner of presenting his gifts was as
delicate and concealed as the measure was large.

Besides this constant course of private dona-
tions, there was scarcely a public charity, or occasion of relief to the ignorant or necessitous,
which did not meet with his distinguished support. His only question was, " May the miseries
of man in any measure be removed or alleviated ?"
Nor was he merely distinguished by stretching
out a liberal hand : his benevolent heart was so
intent on doing good, that he was ever inventing
and promoting plans for its diffusion at home or
abroad.

He who wisely desires any end, will as wisely
regard the means. In this, Mr. Thornton was
perfectly consistent. In order to execute his be-
neficent designs, he observed frugality and exactness in his personal expenses. By such pros-
pective methods he was able to extend the influence of his fortune far beyond those who, in still
more elevated stations, are slaves to expensive
habits. Such men meanly pace in the trammels

of the tyrant custom, till it leaves them scarcely enough to preserve their conscience, or even their credit; much less to employ their talents in Mr. Thornton's nobler pursuits. He, however, could *afford* to be generous, and while he was generous, did not forget his duty in being *just*. He made ample provision for his children: and though, while they are living, it would be indelicate to say more, I am sure of speaking truth, when I say they are so far from thinking themselves impoverished by the bounty of their father, that they contemplate with the highest satisfaction the fruit of those benefits to society which he planted—which it may be trusted will extend with time itself—and which, after his example, they still labor to extend.

But, with all the piety and liberality of this honored character, no man had deeper views of his own unworthiness before his God. To the Redeemer's work alone he looked for acceptance of his person and services: he felt that all he did, or could do, was infinitely short of that which had been done for him, and of the obligations that were thereby laid upon him. It was this abasedness of heart toward God, combined with the most singular largeness of heart toward his fellow-creatures, which distinguished JOHN THORNTON among men.

To this common patron of every useful and pious endeavor, Mr. Newton sent the "Narrative" inserted in the former part of these memoirs. Mr. Thornton replied in his usual manner, that is, by accompanying his letter with a valuable bank note; and, some months after he paid Mr. Newton a visit at Olney. A closer connection being now formed between friends who employed their distinct talents in promoting the same benevolent cause, Mr. Thornton left a sum of money with Mr. Newton to be appropriated to the defraying of his necessary expenses, and the relief of the poor. "Be hospitable," said Mr. Thornton, "and keep an open house for such as are worthy of entertainment. Help the poor and needy. I will statedly allow you 200*l.* a year, and readily send whatever you have occasion to draw for more." Mr. Newton told me, that he thought he had received of Mr. Thornton upward of 3000*l.* in this way during the time he resided at Olney.

The case of most ministers is peculiar, in this respect. Some among them may be looked up to, on account of their publicity and talents: they may have made great sacrifices of their personal interest, in order to enter on their ministry, and may be possessed of the warmest benevolence; but, from the narrowness of their pecuniary circumstances, and from the largeness of their families, they often perceive that an ordinary tradesman in their parishes can subscribe to a charitable or popular institution much more liberally than themselves. This would have been Mr. Newton's case, but for the above-mentioned singular patronage.

A minister, however, should not be so forgetful of his dispensation as to repine at his want of power in this respect. He might as justly estimate his deficiency by the strength of the lion, or the flight of the eagle. The power communicated to *him* is of another kind: and power of every kind belongs to God, who gives gifts to every man severally as he will. The two mites of the widow were all the power of *that* kind which was communicated to her; and her bestowment of her two mites was better accepted than the large offerings of the rich man. The powers, therefore, of Mr. Thornton and of Mr. Newton, though of a different order, were both consecrated to God: and each might have said, *Of thine own have we given thee.*

Providence seems to have appointed Mr. Newton's residence at Olney, among other reasons, for the relief of the depressed mind of the poet COWPER. There has gone forth an unfounded report, that the deplorable melancholy of Cowper was, in part, derived from his residence and connections in that place. The fact, however, is the reverse of this: and, as it may be of importance to the interests of true religion to prevent such a misrepresentation from taking root, I will present the real state of the case, as I have found it attested by the most respectable living witnesses; and, more especially, as confirmed by a MS. written by the poet himself, at the calmest period of his life, with the perusal of which I was favored by Mr. Newton.

It most evidently appears that symptoms of Mr. Cowper's morbid state began to discover themselves in his earliest youth. He seems to have been at all times disordered, in a greater or less degree. He was sent to Westminster school at the age of nine years, and long endured the tyranny of an elder boy, of which he gives an affecting account in the paper above-mentioned; and which "*produced*," as one of his biographers observes, who had long intimacy with him, "*an indelible effect upon his mind through life*." A person so naturally bashful and depressed as Cowper, must needs find the profession of a barrister a further occasion of anxiety. The post obtained for him by his friends in the house of lords overwhelmed him: and the remonstrances which those friends made against his relinquishing so honorable and lucrative an appointment, (but which soon after actually took place,) greatly increased the anguish of a man already incapacitated for business. To all this were added events, which, of themselves, have been found sufficient to overset the strongest minds: namely, the decease of his particular friend and intimate, Sir William Russel; and his meeting with a disappointment in obtaining a lady upon whom his affections were placed.

But the state of a person, torn and depressed (not by his *religious connections*, but) by adverse circumstances, and these meeting a naturally morbid sensibility, *long before he knew Olney, or had formed any connection* with its inhabitants, will best appear from some verses which he sent at this time to one of his female relations, and for the communication of which we are indebted to Mr. Hayley.

> " Doom'd as I am, in solitude to waste
> The present moments, and regret the past ;
> Depriv'd of every joy I valued most,
> My friend torn from me, and my mistress lost:
> Call not this gloom I wear, this anxious mien,
> The dull effect of humor or of spleen !
> Still, still I mourn with each returning day,
> Him—snatch'd by fate, in early youth, away ;
> And her, through tedious years of doubt and pain,
> Fix'd in her choice, and faithful—but in vain.
> See me—ere yet my destin'd course half done,
> Cast forth a wand'rer on a wild unknown !
> See me, neglected on the world's rude coast,
> Each dear companion of my voyage lost !
> Nor ask why clouds of sorrow shade my brow,
> And ready tears wait only leave to flow ;
> Why all that soothes a heart, from anguish free,
> All that delights the happy—palls with me !"

Under such pressures, the melancholy and susceptible mind of Cowper received, from evangelical truth, the first consolation which it ever tasted. It was under the care of Dr. Cotton, of St. Albans, (a physician as capable of administering to the spiritual as to the natural maladies of his patients,) that Mr. Cowper first obtained a clear view of those sublime and animating doctrines which so distinguished and exalted his future strains as a poet. Here, also, he received that settled tranquillity and peace which he enjoyed for several years afterwards. So far, therefore, was his constitutional malady from being produced or increased by his evangelical connections, either at St. Albans or at Olney, that he seems never to have had any settled peace but from the truths he learned in these societies. It appears, that among them alone he found the only sunshine he ever enjoyed through the cloudy day of his afflicted life.

It appears, also, that, while at Dr. Cotton's, Mr. Cowper's distress was for a long time entirely removed, by marking that passage in Rom. 3, 25 : *Him hath God set forth to be a propitiation, through faith in his blood, to declare his righteousness for the remission of sins that are past.* In this scripture he saw the remedy which God provides for the relief of a guilty conscience, with such clearness, that for *several years* after his heart was filled with love, and his life occupied with prayer, praise, and doing good to his needy fellow-creatures.

Mr. Newton told me, that, from Mr. Cowper's first coming to Olney, it was observed he had studied his Bible with such advantage, and was so well acquainted with its design, that not only his troubles were removed, but that, to the end of his life, he never had clearer views of the peculiar doctrines of the Gospel, than when he first became an attendant upon them—that (short intervals excepted) Mr. Cowper enjoyed a course of peace for several successive years—that, during this period, the inseparable attendants of a lively faith appeared, by Mr. Cowper's exerting himself to the utmost of his power in every benevolent service he could render to his poor neighbors—and that Mr. Newton used to consider him as a sort of curate, from his constant attendance upon the sick and afflicted in that large and necessitous parish.

But the malady, which seemed to be subdued by the strong consolations of the Gospel, was still latent; and only required some occasion of irritation, to break out again, and overwhelm the patient. Any object of constant attention that shall occupy a mind previously disordered, whether fear, or love, or science, or religion, will not be so much the CAUSE of the disease, as the accidental OCCASION of exciting it. Cowper's letters will show us how much his mind was occupied at one time by the truths of the Bible, and at another time by the fictions of Homer: but his melancholy was originally a constitutional disease—a physical disorder, which, indeed, could be *affected* either by the Bible or by Homer, but was utterly distinct in its nature from the mere matter of either.

And, here, I cannot but mark this necessary distinction; having often been witness to cases where religion has been assigned as the proper *cause* of insanity, when it has been only an *accidental* occasion, in the case of one *already* affected. Thus COWPER's malady, like a strong current breaking down the banks which had hitherto sustained the pressure and obliquity of its course, prevailed against the supports he had received, and precipitated him again into his former distress.

I inquired of Mr. Newton as to the manner in which Mr. Cowper's disorder returned, after an apparent recovery of nearly nine years' continuance; and was informed that the first symptoms were discovered one morning in his conversation, soon after he had undertaken a new engagement in composition.

As a general and full account of this extraordinary genius is already before the public, such particulars would not have occupied so much room in these memoirs, but with a view of removing the false statements that have been made.

Of great importance also was the vicinity of Mr. Newton's residence to that of the Rev. Thomas Scott, then Curate of Ravenstone and Weston Underwood, and afterwards Rector of Aston Sandford; a man whose ministry and writings have since been so useful to mankind. This clergyman was nearly a Socinian: he was in the habit of ridiculing evangelical religion, and labored to bring over Mr. Newton to his own sentiments. Mr. Scott had married a lady from the family of a Mr. Wright, a gentleman in his parish, who had promised to provide for him. But Mr. Scott's objections to subscription arose so high, that he informed his patron it would be in vain to attempt providing for him in the Church of England; as he could not conscientiously accept a living on the condition of subscribing its Liturgy and Articles. " This," said Mr. Newton, " gave me hopes of Mr. Scott's being sincere, however wrong in his principles."

But the benefit which Mr. Scott derived from his neighbor will best appear in his own words.

"I was," says he, "full of proud self-sufficiency, very positive, and very obstinate: and, being situated in the neighborhood of some of those whom the world calls Methodists, I joined in the prevailing sentiment; held them in sovereign contempt; spoke of them with derision; declaimed against them from the pulpit, as persons full of bigotry, enthusiasm and spiritual pride; laid heavy things to their charge; and endeavored to prove the doctrines which I supposed them to hold (for I had never read their books) to be dishonorable to God, and destructive of morality. And though, in some companies, I chose to conceal part of my sentiments; and, in all, affected to speak as a friend to universal toleration; yet scarcely any person could be more proudly and violently prejudiced against both their persons and principles than I then was.

" In January, 1774, two of my parishioners, a man and his wife, lay at the point of death. I had heard of the circumstance; but, according to my general custom, not being sent for, I took no notice of it: till, one evening, the woman being now dead, and the man dying, I heard that my neighbor, Mr. Newton, had been several times to visit them. Immediately my conscience reproached me with being shamefully negligent, in sitting at home, within a few doors of dying persons, my general hearers, and never going to visit them. Directly it occurred to me, that, whatever contempt I might have for Mr. Newton's *doctrines*, I must acknowledge his *practice* to be more consistent with the ministerial character than my own. He must have more zeal and love for souls than I had, or he would not have walked so far to visit, and supply my lack of care to those who, as far as I was concerned, might have been left to perish in their sins.

"This reflection affected me so much, that, without delay, and very earnestly, yea with tears, I besought the Lord to forgive my past neglect; and I resolved thenceforth to be more attentive to this duty: which resolution, though at first formed in ignorant dependance on my own strength, I have by divine grace been enabled hitherto to keep. I went immediately to visit the survivor; and the affecting sight of one person already dead, and another expiring in the same chamber, served more deeply to impress my serious convictions.

"It was at this time that my correspondence with Mr. Newton commenced. At a visitation, May, 1775, we exchanged a few words on a controverted subject, in the room among the clergy, which I believe drew many eyes upon us. At that time he prudently declined the discourse; but, a day or two after, he sent me a short note, with a little book for my perusal. This was the very thing I wanted: and I gladly embraced the opportunity which, according to my wishes, seemed now to offer; God knoweth, with no in considerable expectations that my arguments would prove irresistibly convincing, and that I should have the honor of rescuing a well-meaning person from his enthusiastical delusions.

" I had, indeed, by this time conceived a very favorable opinion of him, and a sort of respect for him ; being acquainted with the character he sustained even among some persons who expressed a disapprobation of his doctrines. They were forward to commend him as a benevolent, disinterested, inoffensive person, and a laborious minister. But, on the other hand, I looked upon his religious sentiments as rank fanaticism ; and entertained a very contemptuous opinion of his abilities, natural and acquired. Once I had had the curiosity to hear him preach ; and, not understanding his sermon, I made a very great jest of it, where I could do it without giving offence. I had also read one of his publications ; but, for the same reason, I thought the greater part of it whimsical, paradoxical and unintelligible.

" Concealing, therefore, the true motives of my conduct under the offer of friendship and a professed desire to know the truth, (which, a-midst all my self-sufficiency and prejudice, I trust the Lord had even then given me,) with the greatest affectation of candor, and of a mind open to conviction, I wrote him a long letter ; purposing to draw from him such an avowal and explanation

of his sentiments as might introduce a controversial discussion of our religious differences.

"The event by no means answered my expectation. He returned a very friendly and long answer to my letter ; in which he carefully avoided
the mention of those doctrines which he knew
would offend me. He declared that he believed
me to be one who feared God, and was under the
teaching of his Holy Spirit ; that he gladly accepted my offer of friendship, and was nowise inclined to dictate to me : but that, leaving me to
the guidance of the Lord, he would be glad, as
occasion served, from time to time, to bear tes-
timony to the truths of the Gospel; and to communicate his sentiments to me on any subject,
with all the confidence of friendship.

"In this manner our correspondence began :
and it was continued, in the interchange of nine
or ten letters, till December in the same year.
Throughout I held my purpose, and he his. I
made use of every endeavor to draw him into
controversy, and filled my letters with defini-
tions, inquiries, arguments, objections and consequences, requiring explicit answers. He, on the
other hand, shunned every thing controversial as
much as possible, and filled his letters with the
most useful and least offensive instructions : except that, now and then, he dropped his hints
concerning the necessity, the true nature, and

the efficacy of faith, and the manner in which it was to be sought and obtained; and concerning some other matters, suited, as he judged, to help me forward in my inquiry after truth. But they much offended my prejudices, afforded me matter of disputation, and at that time were of little use to me.

" When I had made this little progress in seeking the truth, my acquaintance with Mr. Newton was resumed. From the conclusion of our correspondence, in December, 1775, till April, 1777, it had been almost wholly dropped. To speak plainly, I did not care for his company: I did not mean to make any use of him as an instructor; and I was unwilling the world should think us in any way connected. But, under discouraging circumstances, I had occasion to call upon him; and his discourse so comforted and edified me, that my heart, being by his means relieved from its burden, became susceptible of affection for him. From that time I was inwardly pleased to have him for my friend; though not, as now, rejoiced to call him so. I had, however, even at that time, no thoughts of learning doctrinal truth from him, and was ashamed to be detected in his company; but I sometimes stole away to spend an hour with him. About the same period I once heard him preach, but still it was foolishness to me; his sermon being principally upon the believer's expe-

rience, in some particulars, with which I was un-
acquainted. So that, though I loved and valued
him, I considered him as a person misled by
enthusiastical notions; and strenuously insisted
that we should never think alike till we met in
heaven."*

Mr. Scott, after going on to particularize his
progress in the discovery of truth, and the character of Mr. Newton, as its minister, afterward
adds :

" The pride of reasoning, and the conceit of
superior discernment, had all along accompanied
me : and, though somewhat broken, had yet considerable influence. Hitherto, therefore, I had
not thought of hearing any person preach; because I did not think any one in the circle of my
acquaintance capable of giving me such information as I wanted. But, being at length convinced
that Mr. Newton had been right, and that I had
been mistaken, in the several particulars in which
we had differed, it occurred to me, that, having
preached these doctrines so long, he must understand many things concerning them to which
I was a stranger. Now, therefore, though not
without much remaining prejudice, and not less
in the character of a judge than of a scholar, I

* Scott's Force of Truth.

condescended to be his hearer, and occasionally to attend his preaching, and that of some other ministers. I soon perceived the benefit; for, from time to time the secrets of my heart were discovered to me, far beyond what I had hitherto noticed; and I seldom returned from hearing a sermon, without having conceived a meaner opinion of myself—without having attained to a further acquaintance with my deficiencies, weaknesses, corruptions and wants—or without being supplied with fresh matter for prayer, and directed to greater watchfulness. I likewise learned the use of experience in preaching; and was convinced, that the readiest way to reach the hearts and consciences of others, was to speak from my own. In short, I gradually saw more and more my need of instruction, and was at length brought to consider myself as a very novice in religious matters. Thus I began experimentally to perceive our Lord's meaning, when he says, *Except ye receive the kingdom of heaven as a little child, ye shall in no wise enter therein.*"

In the year 1776 Mr. Newton was afflicted with a tumor or wen, which had formed on his thigh; and, on account of its growing more large and troublesome, he resolved to undergo the experiment of extirpation. This obliged him to go to London for the operation, which was successfully performed, October 10, by the late Mr. Warner, of Guy's hospital. I remember hearing him speak several years afterward of this trying occasion; but the trial did not seem to have affected him as a painful operation, so much as a critical opportunity in which he might fail in demonstrating the patience of a christian under pain. "I felt," said he, "that being enabled to bear a very sharp operation with tolerable calmness and confidence, was a greater favor granted to me than the deliverance from my malady."*

While Mr. Newton thus continued faithfully discharging the duties of his station, and watching for the temporal and eternal welfare of his

* His reflections upon the occasion, in his diary, are as follow:—" Thou didst support me, and make this operation very tolerable. The cure, by thy blessing, was happily expedited; so that on Sunday, the 27th, I was enabled to go to church and hear Mr. F——, and the following Sunday to preach for him. The tenderness and attention of Dr. and Mrs. F——, with whom we were, I cannot sufficiently describe: nor, indeed, the kindness of many other friends. To them I would be thankful, my Lord, but especially to thee; for what are creatures but instruments in thy hand, fulfilling thy pleasure? At home all was preserved quiet, and I met with no incident to distress or disturb me while absent. The last fortnight I preached often, and was hurried about in seeing my friends. But though I had little leisure or opportunity for retirement, and my heart, alas! as usual was sadly reluctant and dull in secret, yet, in public thou wert pleased to favor me with liberty."

flock, a dreadful fire broke out at Olney, October, 1777. Mr. Newton took an active part in comforting and relieving the sufferers; he collected upward of £200 for them; a considerable sum of money, when the poverty and late calamity of the place are considered. Such instances of benevolence toward the people, with the constant assistance he afforded the poor, by the help of Mr. Thornton, naturally led him to expect that he should have so much influence as to restrain gross licentiousness on particular occasions. But to use his own expression, he had "lived to bury the old crop, on which any dependance could be placed." He preached a weekly lecture, which occurred that year on the 5th of November; and, as he feared that the usual way of celebrating it at Olney might endanger his hearers in their attendance at the church, he exerted himself to preserve some degree of quiet on that evening. Instead, however, of hearkening to his entreaties, the looser sort exceeded their former extravagance, drunkenness and rioting, and even obliged him to send out money, to preserve his house from violence. This happened but a year before he finally left Olney. When he related this occurrence to me, he added that he believed he should never have left the place while he lived, had not so incorrigible a spirit prevailed in a parish he had long labored to reform.

But I must remark here, that this is no solitary fact, nor at all unaccountable. The Gospel, we are informed, is not merely "a savor of life unto life," but also "of death unto death." Those whom it does not soften it is often found to harden. Thus we find St. Paul "went into the synagogue and spake boldly for the space of three months, disputing and persuading the things concerning the kingdom of God. But when divers were hardened, and believed not, but spake evil of that way before the multitude, he departed from them."

"The strong man armed" seeks to keep his "house and goods in peace," and if a minister is disposed to let this sleep of death remain, that minister's own house and goods may be permitted to remain in peace also. Such a minister may be esteemed by his parish as a good kind of man—quiet, inoffensive, candid, &c.; and if he discovers any zeal, it is directed to keep the parish in the state he found it; that is, in ignorance and unbelief, worldly-minded, and hard-hearted; the very state of peace in which the strong man armed seeks to keep his palace or citadel, the human heart.

But if a minister, like the subject of these Memoirs, enters into the design of his commission —if he be alive to the interest of his own soul, and that of the souls committed to his charge;

or, as the apostle expresses it, "to save himself and those that hear him," he may depend upon meeting, in his own experience, the truths of that declaration, "Yea, all that will live godly in Christ Jesus shall suffer persecution," in one form of it or another. One of the most melancholy sights we behold is when professed christians, through prejudice, join the world in throwing the stone. There is, however, such a determined enmity to godliness itself in the breast of a certain class of men existing in most parishes, that, whatever learning and good sense is found in their teacher—whatever consistency of character, or blameless deportment he exhibits; whatever benevolence or bounty (like that which Mr Newton exercised at Olney) may constantly appear in his character; such men remain irreconcilable. They will resist every attempt made to appease their enmity. God alone, who changed the hearts of Paul and Newton, can heal these bitter waters.

I recollect to have heard Mr. Newton say on such an occasion, "When God is about to perform any great work, he generally permits some great opposition to it. Suppose Pharaoh had acquiesced in the departure of the children of Israel, or that they had met with no difficulties in the way, they would, indeed, have passed from Egypt to Canaan with ease; but they, as well as the church in all future ages, would have been great losers. The wonder-working God would not have been seen in those extremities which make his arm so visible. A smooth passage here would have made but a poor story."

But under such disorders, Mr. Newton, in no one instance that I ever heard of, was tempted to depart from the line marked out by the precept and example of his Master. He continued to "bless them that persecuted him," knowing that "the servant of the Lord must not strive, but be gentle unto all men, apt to teach, patient." To the last day he spent among them he went straight forward, "in meekness instructing those that opposed, if God peradventure might give them repentance to the acknowledging the truth."

But, before we take a final leave of Olney, the reader must be informed of another part of Mr. Newton's labors. He had published a volume of sermons before he took orders, dated Liverpool, January 1, 1760. In 1762 he published his Omicron, to which his letters, signed Vigil, were afterward annexed. In 1764 appeared his narrative. In 1767 a volume of Sermons, preached at Olney. In 1769 his Review of Ecclesiastical History, and, in 1779, a volume of Hymns, of which some were composed by Mr. Cowper, and distinguished by the letter C prefixed to them. To these succeeded, in 1781, his valuable work, Cardiphonia

From Olney Mr. Newton was removed to the rectory of the united parishes of St. Mary Woolnoth and St. Mary Woolchurch Haw, Lombard-street, on the presentation of his friend, Mr. Thornton.

Some difficulty arose on Mr. Newton's being presented, from Mr. Thornton's right of presentation being claimed by a nobleman; the question was, therefore, at length brought before the house of lords, and determined in favor of Mr. Thornton. Mr. Newton preached his first sermon in these parishes, December 19, 1779, from Eph. 4 : 15, "Speaking the truth in love." It contained an affectionate address to his parishioners, and was directly published for their use.

Here a new and very distinct scene of action and usefulness was set before him. Placed in the centre of London, in an opulent neighborhood, with connections daily increasing, he had now a course of service to pursue, in several respects different from his former at Olney. Being, however, well acquainted with the word of God and the heart of man, he proposed to himself no new weapons of warfare for pulling down the strongholds of sin and Satan around him. He perceived, indeed, most of his parishioners too intent upon their wealth and merchandise to pay much regard to their new minister; but, since they would not come to him, he was determined to go, as far as he could, to them; and, therefore, soon after his institution he sent a printed address to his parishioners: he afterward sent them another address, on the usual prejudices that are taken up against the Gospel. What effects these attempts had then upon them does not appear; certain it is, that these and other acts of his ministry will be recollected by them when the objects of their present pursuits are forgotten or lamented.

I have heard Mr. Newton speak with great feeling on the circumstances of his last important station. "That one," said he, "of the most ignorant, the most miserable, and the most abandoned of slaves, should be plucked from his forlorn state of exile on the coast of Africa, and at length be appointed minister of the parish of the first magistrate of the first city in the world; that he should there not only testify of such grace, but stand up as a singular instance and monument of it; that he should be enabled to record it in his history, preaching and writings, to the world at large—is a fact I can contemplate with admiration, but never sufficiently estimate." This reflection, indeed, was so present to his mind on all occasions and in all places, that he seldom passed a single day any where but he was found referring to the strange event, in one way or other.

When Mr. Newton came to London he resided for some time in Charles' Square, Hoxton; afterward he removed to Coleman-street Buildings, where he continued till his death. Being of the most friendly and communicative disposition, his house was open to christians of all ranks and denominations. Here, like a father among his children, he used to entertain, encourage and instruct his friends, especially younger ministers, or candidates for the ministry. Here also the poor, the afflicted and the tempted, found an asylum and a sympathy which they could scarcely find, in an equal degree, any where besides.

His timely hints were often given with much point and profitable address to the numerous acquaintance who surrounded him in his public station. Some time after Mr. Newton had published his Omicron, and described the three stages of growth in religion, from the blade, the ear, and the full corn in the ear, distinguishing them by the letters A, B, and C, a conceited young minister wrote to Mr. Newton, telling him that he read his own character accurately drawn in that of C. Mr. Newton wrote in reply, that "in drawing the character of C, or full maturity, he had forgotten to add, till now, one prominent feature of C's character, namely, that C never knew his own face."

"It grieves me," said Mr. Newton, "to see so

few of my wealthy parishioners come to church. I always consider the rich as under greater obligations to the preaching of the Gospel than the poor. For at church the rich must hear the whole truth as well as others. There they have no mode of escape. But let them once get home, you will be troubled to get at them; and, when you are admitted, you are so fettered with punctilio, so interrupted and damped with the frivolous conversation of their friends, that, as Archbishop Leighton says, 'it is well if your visit does not prove a blank or a blot.'"

Mr. Newton used to improve every occurrence which he could with propriety bring into the pulpit. One night he found a bill put up at St. Mary Woolnoth's, upon which he largely commented when he came to preach. The bill was to this effect: "A young man having come to the possession of a very considerable fortune, desires the prayers of the congregation that he may be preserved from the snares to which it exposes him." "Now, if the man," said Mr. Newton, "had lost a fortune, the world would not have wondered to have seen him put up a bill, but this man has been better taught."

Coming out of his church on a Wednesday, a lady stopped him on the steps, and said, "The ticket, of which I held a quarter, is drawn a prize of ten thousand pounds. I know you will con-

gratulate me upon the occasion." "Madam,"
said he, "as for a friend under temptation, I will
endeavor to pray for you."

Soon after he came to St. Mary's, I remember
to have heard him say, in a certain company,
"Some have observed that I preach shorter sermons on a Sunday morning, and with more caution; but this I do upon principle. I suppose I
may have two or three of my bankers present,
and some others of my parish, who have hitherto
been strangers to my views of truth. I endeavor
to imitate the apostle. 'I became,' says he, 'all
things to all men;' but observe the end, it was
in order to 'gain some.' The fowler must go
cautiously to meet shy birds, but he will not
leave his powder and shot behind him. 'I have
fed you with milk,' says the apostle; but there
are some that are not only for forcing strong
meat, but bones too, down the throat of the
child. We must have patience with a single step
in the case of an infant; and there are one-step
books and sermons, which are good in their
place. Christ taught his disciples as they were
able to bear; and it was upon the same principle
that the apostle accommodated himself to prejudice. Now," continued he, "what I wish to remark on these considerations is, that this apostolical principle, steadily pursued, will render a
minister apparently inconsistent; superficial hear-

ers will think him a trimmer. On the other hand, a minister, destitute of the apostolical principle and intention, and directing his whole force to preserve the appearance of consistency, may thus seem to preserve it; but, let me tell you, here is only the form of faithfulness without the spirit."

I could not help observing, one day, how much Mr. Newton was grieved with the mistake of a minister who appeared to pay too much attention to politics. "For my part," said he, "I have no temptation to turn politician, and much less to inflame a party in these times. When a ship is leaky, and a mutinous spirit divides the company on board, a wise man would say, 'My good friends, while we are debating the water is gaining on us—we had better leave the debate and go to the pumps.' I endeavor," continued he, "to turn my people's eyes from instruments to God. I am continually attempting to show them how far they are from knowing either the matter of fact or the matter of right. I inculcate our great privileges in this country, and advise a discontented man to take a lodging for a little while in Russia or Prussia."

Though no great variety of anecdote is to be expected in a course so stationary as this part of Mr. Newton's life and ministry—for sometimes the course of a single day might give the account of a whole year—yet that day was so benevolently spent, that he was found in it "not only rejoicing with those that rejoiced," but literally "weeping with those that wept." The portrait which Goldsmith drew from imagination Mr. Newton realized in fact, insomuch that had Mr. Newton sat for his picture to the poet, it could not have been more accurately delineated than by the following lines in his **Deserted Village** :

> " Unskilful he to fawn, or seek for power,
> " By doctrines fashion'd to the varying hour;
> " Far other aims his heart had learn'd to prize,
> " More bent to raise the wretched than to rise.
> " Thus to relieve the wretched was his pride,
> " And e'en his failings lean'd to virtue's side;
> " But in his duty prompt at every call,
> " He watch'd and wept, he pray'd and felt, for all :
> " And as a bird each fond endearment tries
> " To tempt his new-fledged offspring to the skies
> " He tried each art, reprov'd each dull delay,
> " Allur'd to brighter worlds, and led the way."

I remember to have heard him say, when speaking of his continual interruptions, "I see in this world two heaps of human happiness and misery; now if I can take but the smallest bit from one heap and add to the other, I carry a point. If, as I go home, a child has dropped a half-penny, and if, by giving it another, I can wipe away its tears, I feel I have done something. I should be glad indeed to do greater things, but I will not neglect this. When I hear a knock at my study door, I hear a message from God; it may be a lesson of instruction, perhaps a lesson of patience; but since it is his message, it must be interesting."

But it was not merely under his own roof that his benevolent aims were thus exerted; he was found ready to take an active part in relieving the miserable, directing the anxious, or recovering the wanderer, in whatever state or place he discovered such: of which take the following instance:

The late Dr. Buchanan was a youth of considerable talents, and had received a respectable education. I am not informed of his original destination in point of profession; but certain it is, that he left his parents in Scotland, with a design of viewing the world at large; and that, without those pecuniary resources which could render such an undertaking convenient, or even practicable. Yet, having the sanguine expectations of youth, together with its inexperience, he determinately pursued his plan. I have seen an account from his own hand, of the strange, but by no means dishonorable resources to which he was reduced in the pursuit of this scheme; nor can romance exceed the detail. To London, however, he came; and then he seemed to come to himself. He had heard Mr. Newton's character, and on a Sunday evening he came to St. Mary Woolnoth, and stood in one of the aisles while Mr. Newton preached. In the course of that week he wrote to Mr. Newton some account of his adventures and state of mind. Such circumstances could be addressed to no man more properly. Mr. Newton's favorite maxim was often in his mouth, more often in his actions, and always in his heart ;

Haud ignara mali, missris succurrere disco.

" Not ignorant of suffering, I hasten to succor the wretched."

Mr. Newton therefore gave notice from the pulpit on the following Sunday evening, that if the person was present who had sent him such a letter, he should be glad to speak with him.

Mr. Buchanan gladly accepted the invitation, and came to Mr. Newton's house, where a friendship began which continued till Mr. Newton's death. Mr. Newton not only afforded this youth the instruction which he at this period so deeply needed, but marking his fine abilities and correct inclination, he introduced him to Henry Thornton, Esq. who, inheriting his father's unbounded liberality and determined adherence to the cause of real religion, readily patronized the stranger. Mr. Buchanan was, by the munificence of this gentleman, supported through a university education, and was afterward ordained to a curacy. It was, however, thought expedient that his talents should be employed in an important station abroad, which he readily undertook, and in which he maintained a very distinguished character.

It ought not to be concealed that Mr. Buchanan, after his advancement, not only returned his patron the whole expense of his university education, but also placed in his hands an equal sum for the education of some pious youth who might be deemed worthy of the same assistance as was once afforded to himself.

Mr. Newton used to spend a month or two, annually, at the house of some friend in the country; he always took an affectionate leave of his congregation before he departed, and spoke of his leaving town as quite uncertain of returning to it, considering the variety of incidents which might prevent that return. Nothing was more remarkable than his constant habit of regarding the hand of God in every event, however trivial it might appear to others. On every occasion—in the concerns of every hour—in matters public or private, like Enoch, he "walked with God." Take a single instance of his state of mind in this respect. In walking to his church he would say. "'The way of man is not in himself,' nor can he conceive what belongs to a single step—when I go to St. Mary Woolnoth

it seems the same whether I turn down Lothbury
or go through the Old Jewry; but the going
through one street and not another, may produce
an effect of lasting consequences. A man cut
down my hammock in sport, but had he cut it
down half an hour later, I had not been here, as
the exchange of crew was then making. A man
made a smoke on the sea-shore at the time a ship
passed, which was thereby brought to, and af
terward brought me to England."

Mr. Newton experienced a severe stroke soon
after he came to St. Mary's, and while he resided
in Charles Square, in the death of his niece, Miss
Eliza Cunningham. He loved her with the affection of a parent, and she was, indeed, truly lovely.
He had brought her up, and had observed that,
with the most amiable natural qualities, she possessed real piety. With every possible attention
from Mr. and Mrs. Newton and their friends, they
yet saw her gradually sink into the arms of death;
but she was, through grace, prepared to meet him
as a messenger sent from her heavenly Father, to
whom she departed, October 6th, 1785, aged fourteen years and eight months. On this occasion
Mr. Newton published a brief memoir of her character and death.*

---

* This Memoir is Tract No. 83, published by the American Tract Society.

In the years 1784 and 1785 Mr. Newton preached a course of sermons on an occasion of which he gives the following account in his first discourse : " Conversation in almost every company, for some time past, has much turned upon the commemoration of Handel, and particularly on his oratorio of the Messiah. I mean to lead your meditations to the language of the oratorio, and to consider, in their order, (if the Lord, on whom our breath depends, shall be pleased to afford life, ability and opportunity,) the several sublime and interesting passages of Scripture which are the basis of that admired composition." In the year 1786 he published these discourses in two volumes, octavo. There is a passage so original at the beginning of his fourth sermon, from Mal. 3 : 1–3, " The Lord, whom ye seek, shall suddenly come to his temple," &c. that I shall transcribe it for the use of such as have not seen these discourses ; at the same time it will, in a few words, convey Mr. Newton's idea of the usual performance of this oratorio, or attending its performance in present circumstances.

" ' Whereunto shall we liken the people of this generation, and to what are they like ?' " I represent to myself a number of persons, of various characters, involved in one common charge of high treason. They are already in a state of confinement, but not yet brought to their trial

The facts, however, are so plain, and the evidence against them so strong and pointed, that there is not the least doubt of their guilt being fully proved, and that nothing but a pardon can preserve them from punishment. In this situation it should seem their wisdom to avail themselves of every expedient in their power for obtaining mercy: but they are entirely regardless of their danger, and wholly taken up with contriving methods of amusing themselves, that they may pass away the term of their imprisonment with as much cheerfulness as possible. Among other resources, they call in the assistance of music: and amidst a great variety of subjects in this way, they are particularly pleased with one. They choose to make the solemnities of their impending trial, the character of their Judge, the methods of his procedure, and the awful sentence to which they are exposed, the groundwork of a musical entertainment: and, as if they were quite unconcerned in the event, their attention is chiefly fixed upon the skill of the composer, in adapting the style of his music to the very solemn language and subject with which they are trifling. The king, however, out of his great clemency and compassion toward those who have no pity for themselves, prevents them with his goodness. Undesired by them, he sends them a gracious message: he assures them that he is unwilling they should suffer : he requires, yea, he entreats them to submit. He points out a way in which their confession and submission shall be certainly accepted; and in this way, which he condescends to prescribe, he offers them a free and a full pardon. But instead of taking a single step toward a compliance with his goodness, they set his message likewise to music; and this, together with a description of their previous state, and of the fearful doom awaiting them if they continue obstinate, is sung for their diversion, accompanied with the sound of the cornet, flute, harp, sackbut, psaltery, dulcimer, and all kinds of instruments. Surely, if such a case as I have supposed could be found in real life, though I might admire the musical taste of these people, I should commiserate their insensibility."

But " clouds return after the rain :" a greater loss than that of Miss Cunningham was to follow. Enough has been said in these memoirs already to show the more than ordinary affection Mr. Newton felt for her who had been so long his idol, as he used to call her ; of which I shall add but one more instance out of many that might easily be collected.

Being with him at the house of a lady at Blackheath, we stood at a window which had a prospect of Shooter's Hill. "Ah," said Mr. Newton, "I remember the many journeys I took from London to stand at the top of that hill in order to look toward the part in which Mrs. Newton then lived: not that I could see the spot itself, after travelling several miles, for she lived far beyond what I could see when on the hill; but it gratified me even to look toward the spot: and this I did always once, and sometimes twice a week." "Why," said I, "this is more like one of the vagaries of romance than of real life." "True," replied he, "but real life has extravagances that would not be admitted to appear in a well-written romance—they would be said to be out of nature."

In such a continued habit of excessive attachment, it is evident how keenly Mr. Newton must have felt, while he observed the progress of a threatening disorder. This will be manifest from the following account which he published. It was added to his publication, *Letters to a Wife*, and he entitles it

A Relation of some Particulars respecting the Cause, Progress, and Close of the last Illness of my late dear Wife.

"Among my readers there will doubtless be some of a gentle, sympathizing spirit, with whom I am not personally acquainted; and perhaps their feelings may so far interest them in my concerns as to make them not unwilling to read a brief account of my late great trial.

"My dear wife had naturally a good constitution, and was favored with good spirits to the last: but the violent shock she sustained in the year 1754, when I was suddenly attacked by a fit, (I know not of what kind,) which left me no sign of life for about an hour but breathing, made as sudden a change in her habit, and subjected her, from that time, to a variety of chronic complaints. She was several times confined, for five or six months, to her chamber, and often brought so low that her recovery seemed hopeless. I believe she spent ten years, out of the forty that she was spared to me, (if all the days of her sufferings were added together,) in illness and pain. But she had likewise long intervals of health. The fit I have mentioned (the only one I ever had) was the means the Lord was pleased to appoint, in answer to my prayers, to free me from the irksome seafaring life in which I was till then engaged, and to appoint me a settlement on shore.

"Before our removal from Liverpool she received a blow upon her left breast, which occasioned her some pain and anxiety for a little time, but which soon wore off. A small lump remained in the part affected, but I heard no more of it for many years. I believe that, latterly, she felt more than I was aware of; but her tenderness for me made her conceal it as long as possible. I have often since wondered at her success, and how I could be kept so long ignorant of it.

"In the month of October, 1788, she applied, unknown to me, to a friend of mine, an eminent surgeon: her design was, if he approved it, to submit to an operation, and so to adjust time and circumstances with him, that it might be performed in my absence, and before I could know it: but the surgeon told her that the malady was too far advanced, and the tumor (the size of which he compared to the half of a melon) was too large to warrant the hope of being extracted without the most imminent danger of her life, and that he durst not attempt it. He could give her but little advice, more than to keep herself as quiet, and her mind as easy as possible; and little more encouragement, than by saying that the pains to which she was exposed were generally rendered tolerable by the use of laudanum; to which, however, she had a dislike little short of an antipathy.

"I cannot easily describe the composure and resignation with which she gave me this recital the next day after her interview with the surgeon; nor of the sensations of my mind while I heard it. My conscience told me that I had well deserved to be wounded where I was most sensible; and that it was my duty to submit with silence to the will of the Lord. But I strongly felt that, unless he was pleased to give me this submission, I was more likely to toss like a wild bull in a net, in defiance of my better judgment.

" Soon after, the Lord was pleased to visit our dear adopted daughter with a dreadful fever, which at first greatly affected her nerves, and afterward became putrid. She (Miss Catlett) was brought very near to the grave indeed; for we once or twice thought her actually dead. But He, who in the midst of judgment remembers mercy, restored her, and still preserves her, to be the chief temporal comfort of my old age, and to afford me the greatest alleviation of the loss I was soon to experience, that the case could admit.

" The attention and anxiety occasioned by this heavy dispensation, which lasted during the whole of a very severe winter; were by no means suited to promote that tranquillity of mind which my good friend wished my dear wife would endeavor to preserve. She was often much fatigued, and often much alarmed. Next to each other, this dear child had the nearest place, both in her heart and mine. The effect was soon apparent: as the spring of 1789 advanced, her malady rapidly increased; her pains were almost incessant, and often intense, and she could seldom lie one hour in her bed in the same position. Oh! my heart, what didst thou then suffer!

"But in April, the God who heareth prayer mercifully afforded relief, and gave such a blessing to the means employed, that her pains ceased. And though I believe she never had an hour of perfect ease, she felt little of the distressing pains incident to her malady, from that time to the end of her life, (which was about twenty months,) excepting at three or four short intervals, which, taken together, hardly amounted to two hours: and these returns of anguish, I thought, were permitted to show me how much I was indebted to the goodness of God for exempting her feelings and my sympathy from what would have been terrible indeed!

"In the close of the summer she was able to go to Southampton, and returned tolerably well. She was twice at church in the first week after she came home. She then went no more abroad, except in a coach, for a little air and exercise: but she was cheerful, tolerably easy, slept as well as most people who are in perfect health, and could receive and converse with her kind friends who visited her.

"It was not long after, that she began to have a distaste for food, which continued and increased; so that perhaps her death was at last rather owing to weakness, from want of nourishment, than to her primary disorder. Her dislike was, first, to butcher's meat, of which she could bear neither the sight nor the smell. Poultry and fish in their turns became equally distasteful. She retained some relish for small birds awhile after she had given up the rest ; but it was at a season when they were difficult to be obtained. I hope I shall always feel my obligations to the kind friends who spared no pains to procure some for her when they were not to be had in the markets. At that time I set more value upon a dozen of larks than upon the finest ox in Smithfield. But her appetite failed to these also, when they became more plentiful.

"Under this trying discipline I learnt, more sensibly than ever, to pity those whose sufferings, of a similar kind, are aggravated by poverty. Our distress was not small, yet we had every thing within reach that could, in any degree, conduce to her refreshment or relief; and we had faithful and affectionate servants, who were always willingly engaged to their power, yea, as the apostle speaks, beyond their power, in attending and assisting her, by night and by day. What must be the feelings of those who, when afflicted with grievous diseases, pine away, unpitied, unnoticed, without help, and, in a great measure destitute of common necessaries? This reflection, among others, contributed to quiet my mind, and to convince me that I had still much more cause for thankfulness than for complaint.

"For about a twelvemonth of her confinement her spirits were good, her patience was exemplary, and there was a cheerfulness in her looks and her language that was wonderful. Often the liveliness of her remarks has forced a smile from us when the tears were in our eyes. Whatever little contrivances she formed for her amusement, in the course of the day, she would attend to nothing till she had finished her stated reading of the Scripture, in which she employed much time and great attention. I have her Bible by me, (which I would not part with for half the manuscripts in the Vatican,) in which almost every principal text, from the beginning to the end of the book, is marked in the margin with a pencil, by her own dear hand. The good word of God was her medicine and her food, while she was able to read it. She read Dr. Watts' Psalms and Hymns, and the Olney Hymns, in the same manner. There are few of them in which one, two, or more verses, are not thus marked; and in many, which I suppose she read more frequently, every verse is marked.

"But in October the enemy was permitted, for a while, to take advantage of her bodily weakness, to disturb the peace and serenity of her mind. Her thoughts became clouded and confused; and she gradually lost, not only the comfortable evidence of her own interest in the precious truths of the Bible, but she lost all hold of the truth itself. She doubted the truth of the Bible, or whether truth existed; and, together with this, she expressed an extreme reluctance to death, and could not easily bear the most distant hint of her approaching end, though we were expecting it daily and hourly. This was the *acme*, the highwater-mark of my trial: this was hard to bear indeed.

"My readers, perhaps, will scarcely believe that I derived some consolation, during this period, from perceiving that her attachment to me was very sensibly abated. She spoke to me with an indifference, of which, a little before, she was incapable. If, when the Lord's presence was withdrawn, and she could derive no comfort from his word, she had found some relief from my being with her, or from hearing me speak, I should have been more grieved. Her affection to me, confirmed by so many proofs, in the course of forty years, was not to be impeached by this temporary suspension of its exercise. I judged the same of the frame of her mind, as to her spiritual concerns: I ascribed them both to the same cause—her bodily weakness, and the power of temptation. She was relieved, in both respects, after about a fortnight spent in conflict and dismay. The Lord restored peace to her soul, and then her former tenderness to me immediately revived. Then, likewise, she could calmly speak of her approaching dissolution. She mentioned some particulars concerning her funeral, and our domestic concerns, with great composure. But her mind was not so fully restored to its former tone as to give her freedom to enlarge upon her hopes and views, as I had wished, till near her dissolution; and then she was too low to speak at all.

"One addition to our trial yet remained. It had been her custom, when she went from her sofa to her bed, to exert herself for my encouragement, to show me how well she could walk. But it pleased the Lord that, by some alteration, which affected her spine, she was disabled from moving herself; and other circumstances rendered it extremely difficult to move her. It has taken five of us nearly two hours to remove her from one side of the bed to the other, and, at times, even this was impracticable: so that she has lain more than a week exactly in the same spot, without the possibility of changing her position. All this was necessary on my account. The rod had a voice, and it was the voice of the Lord. I understood the meaning no less plainly than if he had spoken audibly from heaven, and said, "Now contemplate your idol. Now see what *she* is

whom you once presumed to prefer to *Me!*"
Even this bitter cup was sweetened by the patience and resignation which he gave her. When
I have said, "You suffer greatly," her answer
usually was, "I suffer, indeed, but not greatly."
And she often expressed her thankfulness that,
though her body was immoveable, she was still
permitted the use of her hands.

"One of the last sensible concerns she felt,
respecting *this* world, was when my honored
friend, patron and benefactor, the late John
Thornton, Esq. of Clapham, was removed to a
better. She revered and regarded him, I believe,
more than she did any person upon earth: and
she had reason. Few had nearer access to know
and admire his character; and perhaps none
were under greater, if equal, obligations to him
than we. She knew of his illness, but was always
afraid to inquire after the event; nor should I
have ventured to inform her, but that the occasion requiring me to leave her for four or five
hours, when I hardly expected to find her alive
at my return, I was constrained to give her the
reason of my absence. She eagerly replied, "Go
by all means; I would not have you stay with
me upon any consideration." I put the funeral
ring I was favored with into her hands; she put
it first to her lips, and then to her eyes, bedew-
ing it with her tears. I trust they soon met

again. But she survived him more than a month.

"Her head became so affected that I could do little more than sit and look at her. Our intercourse by words was nearly broken off. She could not easily bear the sound of the gentlest foot upon the carpet, nor of the softest voice On Sunday, the 12th of December, when I was preparing for church in the morning, she sent for me, and we took a final farewell, as to this world. She faintly uttered an endearing appellation, which was familiar to her, and gave me her hand, which I held, while I prayed by her bedside. We exchanged a few tears; but I was almost as unable to speak as she was. But I returned soon after, and said, 'If your mind, as I trust, is in a state of peace, it will be a comfort to me if you can signify it by holding up your hand.' She held it up, and waved it to and fro several times.

"That evening her speech, her sight, and I believe, her hearing, wholly failed. She continued perfectly composed, without taking notice of any thing, or discovering any sign of pain or uneasiness, till Wednesday evening toward seven o'clock. She then began to breathe very hard; her breathing might be called groaning, for it was heard in every part of the house; but I believe it was entirely owing to the difficulty of respiration, for she lay quite still, with a placid countenance, as if in a gentle slumber. There was no start or struggle, nor a feature ruffled. I took my post by her bed-side, and watched her nearly three hours, with a candle in my hand, till I saw her breathe her last, on the 15th of December, 1790, a little before ten in the evening.

"When I was sure she was gone I took off her ring, according to her repeated injunction, and put it upon my own finger. I then kneeled down with the servants who were in the room, and returned the Lord my unfeigned thanks for her deliverance, and her peaceful dismission.

"How wonderful must be the moment after death! What a transition did she then experience! She was instantly freed from sin, and all its attendant sorrows, and, I trust, instantly admitted to join the heavenly choir. That moment was remarkable to me likewise. It removed from me the chief object which made another day or hour of life, as to my own personal concern, desirable. At the same time it set me free from a weight of painful feelings and anxieties, under which nothing short of a divine power could have so long supported me.

"I believe it was about two or three months before her death, when I was walking up and down the room, offering disjointed prayers from a heart torn with distress, that a thought suddenly struck me with unusual force, to this effect: The promises of God must be true; surely the

Lord will help me, *if I am willing to be helped!*
It occurred to me that we are often led, from a
vain complacence in what we call our sensibility,
to indulge that unprofitable grief which both our
duty and our peace require us to resist to the utmost of our power. I instantly said aloud, ' Lord,
I am helpless indeed in myself, but I hope I am
willing, without reserve, that thou shouldst help
me.'

" It had been much upon my mind, from the
beginning of this trial, that I was a minister, and
that the eyes of many were upon me ; that my
turn of preaching had very much led me to endeavor to comfort the afflicted, by representing
the Gospel as a catholicon, affording an effectual
remedy for every evil, a full compensation for
every want or loss to those who truly receive it ;
so that though a believer may be afflicted, he
cannot be properly unhappy, unless he gives way
to self-will and unbelief. I had often told my
hearers that a state of trial, if rightly improved,
was, to the christian, a post of honor, affording
the fairest opportunity of exemplifying the power of divine grace, to the praise and glory of the
Giver. It had been, therefore, my frequent daily
prayer that I might not, by impatience or despondency, be deprived of the advantage my
situation afforded me, of confirming by my own
practice the doctrine which I had preached to

others; and that I might not give them occasion to apply to me the words of Eliphaz to Job, chap. 4 : 4, 5, " Thy words have upholden him that was falling, and thou hast strengthened the feeble knees; but now it is come upon thee, and thou faintest; it toucheth thee, and thou art troubled!" And I had not prayed in vain. But from the time that I so remarkably felt myself *willing to be helped*, I might truly say, to the praise of the Lord my heart trusted in him, and I was helped indeed. Through the whole of my painful trial I attended all my stated and occasional services as usual; and a stranger would scarcely have discovered, either by my words or looks, that I was in trouble. Many of our intimate friends were apprehensive that this long affliction, and especially the closing event, would have over-whelmed me; but it was far otherwise. It did not prevent me from preaching a single sermon, and I preached on the day of her death.

" After she was gone, my willingness to be helped, and my desire that the Lord's goodness to me might be observed by others, for their en-couragement, made me indifferent to some laws of established custom, the breach of which is often more noticed than the violation of God's commands. I was afraid of sitting at home, and indulging myself, by poring over my loss; and therefore I was seen in the street, and visited some of my serious friends the very next day I likewise preached three times while she lay dead in the house. Some of my brethren kindly offered their assistance; but as the Lord was pleased to give me strength, both of body and mind, I thought it my duty to stand up in my place as formerly. And after she was deposited in the vault I preached her funeral sermon,* with little more sensible emotion than if it had been for another person. I have reason to hope that many of my hearers were comforted and animated under their afflictions, by what they saw of the Lord's goodness to me in my time of need. And I acknowledge that it was well worth standing a while in the fire, for such an opportunity of experiencing and exhibiting the power and faithfulness of his promises.

"I was not supported by lively sensible consolations, but by being enabled to realize to my mind some great and leading truths of the word of God. I saw, what indeed I knew before, but never till then so strongly and clearly perceived, that, as a sinner, I had no *right*, and as a believer, I could have no *reason* to complain. I considered her as a loan, which He who lent her to me had a right

* From a text which I had reserved from my first entrance on the ministry, for this particular service, if I should survive her, and be able to speak.

to resume whenever he pleased; and that as I had deserved to forfeit her every day, from the first, it became me rather to be thankful that she was spared so long to me, than to resign her with reluctance when called for. Farther, that his sovereignty was connected with infinite wisdom and goodness, and that, consequently, if it were possible for me to alter any part of his plan, I could only spoil it; that such a short-sighted creature as I, so blind to the possible consequences of my own wishes, was not only unworthy, but unable to choose well for himself; and that it was therefore my great mercy and privilege that the Lord condescended to choose for me. May such considerations powerfully affect the hearts of my readers under their troubles, and then I shall not regret having submitted to the view of the public a detail which may seem more proper for the subject of a private letter to a friend. They who can feel, will, I hope, excuse me: and it is chiefly for their sakes that I have written it.

When my wife died the world seemed to die with her, (I hope, to revive no more.) I see little now but my ministry and my christian profession to make a continuance in life for a single day desirable; though I am willing to wait my appointed time. If the world cannot restore *her* to me (not that I have the remotest wish that her return

was possible) it can do nothing for me. The
Bank of England is too poor to compensate for
such a loss as mine. But the Lord, the all-suffi-
cient God, speaks, and it is done. Let those who
know him, and trust him, be of good courage.
He can give them strength according to their
day; he can increase their strength as their
trials are increased, to any assignable degree.
And what he *can* do, he has promised he *will* do.
The power and faithfulness on which the successive changes of day and night, and of the
seasons of the year depend, and which uphold
the stars in their orbits, are equally engaged to
support his people, and to lead them safely and
unhurt (if their path be so appointed) through
floods and flames. Though I believe she has
never yet been (and probably never will be) out
of my waking thoughts for five minutes at a
time, though I sleep in the bed in which she suffered and languished so long, I have not had one
uncomfortable day, nor one restless night since
she left me. I have lost a right hand, which I
cannot but miss continually, but the Lord enables
me to go on cheerfully without it.

"May his blessing rest upon the reader! May
glory, honor and praise be ascribed to his great
and holy name, now and for ever! Amen."

Lines composed by Mr. Newton, and sung after the funeral sermon of Mrs. Newton.

HABAKKUK, 3 : 17, 18

" The earth, with rich abundance stor'd,
  To answer all our wants,
Invites our hearts to praise the Lord
  For what his bounty grants.

" Flocks, herds and corn, and grateful fruit,
  His gracious hand supplies ;
And while our various tastes they suit,
  Their prospect cheers our eyes.

" To these he adds each tender tie
  Of sweet domestic life ;
Endearing joys, the names imply,
  Of parent, husband, wife.

" But sin has poisoned all below ;
  Our blessings burdens prove ;
On ev'ry hand we suffer wo,
  But most where most we love.

" Nor vintage, harvest, flocks nor herds,
  Can fill the heart's desire ;
And oft a worm destroys our gourds,
  And all our hopes expire.

" Domestic joys, alas ! how rare !
  Possessed and known by few !
And they who know them, find they are
  As frail and transient too.

" But you who love the Savior's voice,
  And rest upon his name,
Amidst these changes may rejoice,
  For he is still the same.

" The Lord himself will soon appear
  Whom you, unseen, adore ;
Then he will wipe off every tear,
  And you shall weep no more."

    Mr. Newton made this remark on her death,
" Just before Mrs. Newton's disease became so
formidable, I was preaching on the waters of
Egypt being turned into blood. The Egyptians
had idolized their river, and God made them
loath it. I was apprehensive it would soon be a
similar case with me." During the very affecting season of Mrs. Newton's dissolution, Mr.
Newton, like David, wept and prayed; but the
desire of his eyes being taken away by the
stroke, he too, like David, "arose from the
earth, and came into the temple of the Lord, and
worshipped," and that in a manner which surprised some of his friends.

    Besides which, Mr. Newton had a favorite sen-
timent which I have heard him express in different ways, long before he had so special an occasion for illustrating it in practice. "God, in his
providence," he used to say, "is continually
bringing about occasions to demonstrate characters." He used to instance the case of Achan
and Judas among bad men ; and that of St. Paul,

Acts, 27, among good ones. "If any one," said he, "had asked the centurion who Paul the prisoner was that sailed with them on board the ship? it is probable he would have thus replied, ' He is a troublesome enthusiast, who has lately joined himself to a certain sect. These people affirm that a Jewish malefactor, who was crucified some years ago at Jerusalem, rose the third day from the dead; and this Paul is mad enough to assert that Jesus, the leader of their sect, is not only now alive, but that he himself has seen him, and is resolved to live and die with him— Poor crazy creature!' But God made use of this occasion to discover the real character of Paul, and taught the centurion, from the circumstances which followed, to whom it was he owed his direction in the storm, and for whose sake he received his preservation through it."

In all trying occasions, therefore, Mr. Newton was particularly impressed with the idea of a christian, and especially of a christian minister, being called to stand forward as an example to his flock—to feel himself placed in a post of honor—a post in which he may not only glorify God, but also forcibly demonstrate the peculiar supports of the Gospel. More especially when this could be done (as in his own case) from no doubtful motive; then it may be expedient to leave the path of ordinary custom, for the greater reason of exhibiting both the doctrines of truth and the experience of their power.

Though I professedly publish none of Mr. Newton's letters, yet I shall take the liberty to insert part of one, with which I am favored by J. Forbes, Esq. of Stanmore Hill, written to him while at Rome, and dated December 5th, 1796. It shows the interest which the writer took in the safety of his friend, and his address in attempting to break the enchantments with which men of taste are surrounded, when standing in the centre of the fine arts.

"The true christian, in strict propriety of speech, has no home here; he is, and must be, a stranger and a pilgrim upon earth: his citizenship, treasure and real home, are in a better world; and every step he takes, whether to the east or to the west, is a step nearer to his Father's house. On the other hand, when in the path of duty, he is always at home; for the whole earth is the Lord's: and as we see the same sun in England or Italy, in Europe or Asia, so wherever he is, he equally sets the Lord always before him, and finds himself equally near the throne of grace at all times and in all places. God is every where, and, by faith in the great Mediator, he dwells in God, and God in him." To him that line of Horace may be applied in the best sense,

Cœlum, non animum mutant, qui trans mare currunt.*

"I trust, my dear sir, that you will carry out and bring home with you, a determination similar to that of the patriarch Jacob, who vowed a vow, saying, 'If God will be with me, and will keep me in the way that I go, and will give me bread to eat, and raiment to put on, so that I come again to my father's house in peace, then shall the Lord be my God!' May the Lord himself write it on your heart!

"You are now at Rome, the centre of the fine arts; a place abounding with every thing to gratify a person of your taste. Athens had the preeminence in the apostle Paul's time; and I think it highly probable, from many passages in his writings, that he likewise had a taste capable of admiring and relishing the beauties of painting, sculpture and architecture, which he could not but observe during his abode in that city: but then he had a higher, a spiritual, a divine taste, which was greatly shocked and grieved by the ignorance, idolatry and wickedness, which surrounded him, insomuch that he could attend to nothing else. This taste, which cannot be acquired by any effort or study of ours, but is freely bestowed on all who sincerely ask it of

---

* They who cross the ocean change their sky but not the emotions of the soul.

the Lord, divests the vanities, which the world admire, of their glare; and enables us to judge of the most splendid and specious works of men, who know not God, according to the declaration of the prophet, 'They hatch cockatrice eggs, and weave the spider's web.' Much ingenuity is displayed in the weaving of a cobweb, but when finished, it is worthless and useless: incubation requires close diligence and attention; if the hen is too long from her nest, the egg is spoiled; but why should she sit at all upon the egg, and watch it, and warm it night and day, if it only produces a cockatrice at last? Thus vanity and mischief are the chief rulers of unsanctified genius; the artists spin webs, and the philosophers, by their learned speculations, hatch cockatrices, to poison themselves and their fellow-creatures: few of either sort have one serious thought of that awful eternity upon the brink of which they stand for a while, and into the depth of which they successively fall.

"A part of the sentence denounced against the city, which once stood upon seven hills, is so pointed and graphical that I must transcribe it: 'And the voice of harpers, and musicians, and pipers, and trumpeters, shall be heard no more at all in thee; and no craftsman, of whatsoever craft he be, shall be found any more in thee, and the light of a candle shall no more be seen in thee.' Now, I am informed, that upon certain occasions the whole cupola of St. Peter's is covered with lamps, and affords a very magnificent spectacle: if I saw it, it would remind me of that time when there will not be the shining of a single candle in the city; for the sentence must be executed, and the hour may be approaching.

"You kindly inquire after my health : myself and family are, through the Divine favor, perfectly well; yet, healthy as I am, I labor under a growing disorder, for which there is no cure ; I mean old age. I am not sorry it is a mortal disease, from which no one recovers ; for who would live always in such a world as this, who has a Scriptural hope of an inheritance in the world of light ? I am now in my seventy-second year, and seem to have lived long enough for myself ; I have known something of the evil of life, and have had a large share of the good. I know what the world can do, and what it cannot do ; it can neither give nor take away that peace of God which passeth all understanding; it cannot sooth a wounded conscience, nor enable us to meet death with comfort. That you, my dear sir, may have an abiding and abounding experience that the Gospel is a catholicon, adapted to all our wants and all our feelings, and a suitable help when every other help fails, is the sincere and ardent prayer of your affectionate friend," &c.

But in proportion as Mr. Newton felt the vanity of earthly pursuits, he was as feelingly alive to whatever regarded eternal concerns. Take an instance of this in a visit which he paid another friend. This friend was a minister who affected great accuracy in his discourses, and who, on that Sunday, had nearly occupied an hour in insisting on several labored and nice distinctions made in his subject. As he had a high estimation of Mr. Newton's judgment, he inquired of him, as they walked home, whether he thought the distinctions just now insisted on were full and judicious? Mr. Newton said he thought them not full, as a very important one had been omitted. "What can that be?" said the minister, "for I had taken more than ordinary care to enumerate them fully." "I think not," replied Mr. Newton, "for when many of your congregation had travelled several miles for a meal, I think you should not have forgotten the important distinction which must ever exist between meat and bones."

In the year 1799 Mr. Newton had the honorary degree of D. D. conferred upon him by the university of New Jersey, in America, and the diploma sent him. He also received a work in two volumes, dedicated to him, with the above title annexed to his name. Mr. Newton wrote the author a grateful acknowledgment for the work, but begged to decline an honor which he never intended to accept. "I am," said he, "as one born out of due time.* I have neither the pretension nor wish to honors of this kind. However, therefore, the university may over-rate my attainments, and thus show their respect, I must not forget myself; it would be both vain and improper were I to concur in it."

But Mr. Newton had yet another storm to weather. While we were contemplating the long and rough voyage he had passed, and thought he

---

* In a MS. note on a letter dated 15th Dec. 1797, he writes, "Though I am not so sensibly affected as I could wish, I hope I am truly affected by the frequent reviews I make of my past life. Perhaps the annals of Thy church scarcely afford an instance in all respects so singular. Perhaps Thy grace may have recovered some from an equal degree of apostacy, infidelity and profligacy: but few of them have been redeemed from such a state of misery and depression as I was in, upon the coast of Africa, when thy unsought mercy wrought for my deliverance: but that such a wretch should not only be spared, and pardoned, but reserved to the honor of preaching Thy Gospel, which he had blasphemed and renounced, and at length be placed in a very public situation, and favored with acceptance and usefulness, both from the pulpit and the press, so that my poor name is known in most parts of the world where there are any who know Thee— this is wonderful indeed! The more Thou hast exalted me, the more I ought to abase myself."

had only now to rest in a quiet haven, and with a fine sunsetting at the close of the evening of his life; clouds began to gather again, and seemed to threaten a wreck at the very entry of the port.

He used to make excursions in the summer to different friends in the country, endeavoring to make these visits profitable to them and their neighbors, by his continual prayers, and the expositions he gave of the Scriptures read at their morning and evening worship: I have heard of some who were first brought to the knowledge of themselves and of God by attending his exhortations on these occasions; for, indeed, besides what he undertook in a more stated way at the church, he seldom entered a room but something both profitable and entertaining fell from his lips. After the death of Miss Cunningham and Mrs. Newton, his companion in these summer excursions was his other niece, Miss Elizabeth Catlett. This young lady had also been brought up by Mr. and Mrs. Newton with Miss Cunningham, and on the death of the two latter, she became the object of Mr. Newton's naturally affectionate disposition. She also became quite necessary to him by her administrations in his latter years; she watched him, walked with him, visited whereever he went; when his sight failed she read to him, divided his food, and was unto him all that a dutiful daughter could be.

But in the year 1801 a nervous disorder seized her, by which Mr. Newton was obliged to submit to her being separated from him. During the twelvemonth it lasted, the weight of the affliction, added to his weight of years, seemed to overwhelm him. I extracted a few of his reflections on the occasion, written on some blank leaves in an edition of his Letters to a Wife, which he lent me on my undertaking these Memoirs, and subjoin them in a note.* It may give the reader

* "August 1st, 1801. I now enter my 77th year. I have been exercised this year with a trying and unexpected change; but it is by thy appointment, my gracious Lord; and thou art unchangeably wise, good and merciful. Thou gavest me my dear adopted child. Thou didst own my endeavors to bring her up for thee. I have no doubt that thou hast called her by thy grace. I thank thee for the many years' comfort (ten) I have had in her, and for the attention and affection she has always shown me, exceeding that of most daughters to their own parents. Thou hast now tried me, as thou didst Abraham, in my old age; when my eyes are failing, and my strength declines. Thou hast called for my Isaac, who had so long been my chief stay and staff, but it was thy chief blessing that made her so. A nervous disorder has seized her, and I desire to leave her under thy care; and chiefly pray for myself, that I may be enabled to wait thy time and will, without betraying any signs of impatience or despondency unbecoming my profession and character. Hitherto thou hast helped me; and to thee I look for help in future. Let all issue in thy glory, that my friends and hearers may be encouraged by seeing how I am supported; let thy strength be manifest in my weakness, and thy grace

pleasure to be informed that Miss Catlett returned home and gradually recovered.*

It was with a mixture of delight and surprise
that the friends and hearers of this eminent servant of God beheld him bringing forth such a
measure of fruit in extreme age. Though then almost eighty years old, his sight nearly gone, and
incapable, through deafness, of joining in conversation, his public ministry was regularly continued, and maintained with a considerable degree
of his former animation. His memory, indeed,
was observed to fail, but his judgment in divine
things still remained; and though some depression of spirits was observed, which he used to
account for from his advanced age, his percep-
tion, taste and zeal for the truths he had long received and taught, were evident. Like Simeon,
having seen the salvation of the Lord, he now
only waited and prayed to depart in peace.

be sufficient for me, and let all finally work together for our
good. Amen. I aim to say from my heart, Not my will, but
thine, be done. But though thou hast in a measure made my
spirit willing, thou knowest, and I feel, that the flesh is
weak. Lord, I believe, help thou my unbelief. Lord, I submit, subdue every rebellious thought that dares arise against
thy will. Spare my eyes, if it please thee: but, above all,
strengthen my faith and love."

* Mr. Newton's Letters to an Adopted Daughter were
written to her: they are published bv the American Tract
Society.

After Mr. Newton was turned of eighty some of his friends feared he might continue his public ministrations too long; they marked not only his infirmities in the pulpit, but felt much on account of the decrease of his strength and of his occasional depressions. Conversing with him in January, 1806, on the latter, he observed that he had experienced nothing which in the least affected the principles he had felt and taught; that his depressions were the natural result of fourscore years, and that, at any age, we can only enjoy that comfort from our principles which God is pleased to send. "But," replied I, "in the article of public preaching, might it not be best to consider your work as done, and stop before you evidently discover you can speak no longer?" "I cannot stop," said he, raising his voice; "What! shall the old African blasphemer stop while he can speak?"

In every future visit I perceived old age making rapid strides. At length his friends found some difficulty in making themselves known to him: his sight, his hearing and his recollection exceedingly failed; but, being mercifully kept from pain, he generally appeared easy and cheerful. Whatever he uttered was perfectly consistent with the principles he had so long and so honorably maintained. Calling to see him a few days before he died, with one of his most inti-

mate friends, we could not make him recollect
either of us; but seeing him afterward, when sitting up in his chair, I found as much intellect
remaining as produced a short and affectionate
reply, though he was utterly incapable of conversation.

Mr. Newton declined in this very gradual way,
till at length it was painful to ask him a question,
or attempt to rouse faculties almost gone; still
his friends were anxious to get a word from him,
and those friends who survive him will be as
anxious to learn the state of his mind in his
latest hours. It is quite natural thus to inquire,
though it is not important how such a decided
character left this world. I have heard Mr. Newton say, when he has heard particular inquiry
made about the last expressions of an eminent
believer, " Tell me not how the man died, but
how he lived."

Still I say it is natural to inquire, and I will
meet the desire (not by trying to expand un-
interesting particulars, but) as far as I can collect encouraging facts; and I learn, from a paper kindly sent me by his family, all that is interesting and authentic.

About a month before Mr. Newton's death, Mr.
Smith's niece was sitting by him, to whom he
said, " It is a great thing to die; and when flesh
and heart fail, to have God for the strength of

our heart, and our portion for ever: I know whom I have believed, and he is able to keep that which I have committed unto him against that day. Henceforth there is laid up for me a crown of righteousness, which the Lord, the righteous Judge, shall give me at that day."

When Mrs. Smith (his niece, formerly Miss Catlett) came into the room, he said, "I have been meditating on a subject, 'Come and hear, all ye that fear God, and I will declare what he hath done for my soul.'"

At another time he said, "More light, more love, more liberty—Hereafter I hope, when I shut my eyes on the things of time, I shall open them in a better world. What a thing it is to live under the shadow of the wings of the Almighty! I am going the way of all flesh." And when one replied, "The Lord is gracious," he answered, "If it were not so, how could I dare to stand before him?"

The Wednesday before he died Mrs. G—— asked him if his mind was comfortable; he replied, "I am satisfied with the Lord's will."

Mr. Newton seemed sensible to his last hour, but expressed nothing remarkable after these words. He departed on the 21st, and was buried in the vault of his church, the 31st of December, 1807, having left the following injunction, in a letter, for the direction of his executors:

"I propose writing an epitaph for myself, if it may be put up, on a plain marble tablet, near the vestry-door, to the following purport:

JOHN NEWTON, CLERK,
Once an Infidel and Libertine,
A servant of slaves in Africa,
Was, by the rich mercy of our Lord and Savior
JESUS CHRIST,
Preserved, restored, pardoned,
And appointed to preach the Faith,
(He had long labored to destroy,)
Near sixteen years at Olney, in Bucks,
And .. years in this church.
On Feb. 1, 1750, he married
MARY,
Daughter of the late George Catlett,
Of Chatham, Kent.
He resigned her to the Lord who gave her,
On the 15th of December, 1790.

"And I earnestly desire that no other monument, and no inscription but to this purport, may be attempted for me."

The following is a copy of the beginning of Mr. Newton's will, dated June 13, 1803:

"In the name of God, Amen. I, JOHN NEWTON, of Coleman-street Buildings, in the parish of St. Stephen, Coleman-street, in the city of London, Clerk, being, through mercy, in good health and of sound and disposing mind, memory and understanding, although in the seventy-eighth year of my age, do, for the settling of my temporal concerns, and for the disposal of all the worldly estate which it hath pleased the Lord in his good providence to give me, make this my last Will and Testament as follows. I commit my soul to my gracious God and Savior, who mercifully spared and preserved me when I was an apostate, a blasphemer and an infidel; and delivered me from that state of misery on the coast of Africa into which my obstinate wickedness had plunged me; and who has been pleased to admit me (though most unworthy) to preach his glorious Gospel. I rely with humble confidence upon the atonement and mediation of the Lord Jesus Christ, God and man, which I have often proposed to others as the only foundation whereon a sinner can build his hope; trusting that he will guard and guide me through the uncertain remainder of my life, and that he will then admit me into his presence in his heavenly kingdom. I would have my body deposited in the vault under the parish church of Saint Mary Woolnoth, close to the coffins of my late dear wife and my dear niece, Elizabeth Cunningham; and it is my desire that my funeral may be performed with as little expense as possible, consistent with decency."

MR. NEWTON'S CHARACTER

There seems to be little need of giving a general character of Mr. Newton after the particulars which appear in the foregoing memoirs. He
unquestionably was the child of a peculiar providence, in every step of his progress; and his deep
sense of the extraordinary dispensation through
which he had passed was the prominent topic in
his conversation. Those who personally knew
the man, could have no doubt of the probity with
which his " Narrative " (singular as it may appear) was written. They, however, who could
not view the subject of these memoirs so nearly
as his particular friends did, may wish to learn
something further of his character with respect
to his LITERARY ATTAINMENTS—his MINISTRY—his
FAMILY HABITS—his WRITINGS—and his FAMILIAR
CONVERSATION.

Of his LITERATURE, we learn from his " Narrative " what he attained in the learned languages;
and that, by almost incredible efforts. Few men
have undertaken such difficulties under such disadvantages. It, therefore, seems more extraordinary that he should have attained so much, than
that he should not have acquired more. Nor did
he quit his pursuits of this kind, but in order to

gain that knowledge which he deemed much more important. Whatever he conceived had a tendency to qualify him, as *a scribe well instructed in the kingdom of God, bringing out of his treasury things new and old*—I say, in pursuit of *this* point, he might have adopted the apostle's expression, *One thing I do.* By a principle so simply and firmly directed, he furnished his mind with much information: he had consulted the best old divines; had read the moderns of reputation with avidity; and was continually watching whatever might serve for analogies or illustrations in the service of religion. " A minister," he used to say, " wherever he is, should be always in his study. He should look at every man, and at every thing, as capable of affording him some instruction." His mind, therefore, was ever intent on his calling—ever extracting something even from the basest materials which he could turn into gold.

In consequence of this incessant attention to this object, while many (whose early advantages greatly exceeded his) might excel Mr. Newton in the knowledge and investigation of some curious abstract, but very unimportant points; he vastly excelled them in points of infinitely higher importance to man:—In the knowledge of God, of his word, and of the human heart in its wants and resources, Newton would have stood among

mere scholars, as his namesake the philosopher
stood in science among ordinary men. I might
say the same of some others who have set out
late in the profession; but who, with a portion
of Mr. Newton's piety and ardor, have greatly
outstripped those who have had every early advantage and encouragement: men with specious
titles and high connections have received the *re-
wards;* while men, like Newton, without them,
have done the *work.*

With respect to his MINISTRY, he appeared, perhaps, to least advantage in the pulpit; as he did
not generally aim at accuracy in the *composition*
of his sermons, nor at any *address* in the delivery
of them. His utterance was far from clear, and
his attitudes ungraceful. He possessed, however,
so much affection for his people, and so much
zeal for their best interests, that the defect of
his manner was of little consideration with his
constant hearers: at the same time, his capacity
and habit of entering into their trials and experience, gave the highest interest to his ministry
among them. Besides which, he frequently
interspersed the most brilliant allusions; and
brought forward such happy illustrations of his
subject, and those with so much unction, on his
own heart, as melted and enlarged theirs. The
parent-like tenderness and affection which accompanied his instruction, made them prefer him

to preachers, who, on other accounts, were much more generally popular.

It ought also to be noted, that, amidst the extravagant notions and unscriptural positions which have sometimes disgraced the religious world, Mr. Newton never departed, in any instance, from soundly and seriously promulgating the *faith once delivered to the saints;* of which his writings will remain the best evidence. His doctrine was strictly that of the Church of England, urged on the consciences of men in the most practical and experimental manner. "I hope," said he one day to me, smiling, "I hope I am, upon the whole, a SCRIPTURAL preacher; for I find I am considered as an Armenian among the high Calvinists, and as a Calvinist among the strenuous Armenians."

I never observed any thing like bigotry in his ministerial character; though he seemed, at all times, to appreciate the beauty of order and its good effects in the ministry. He had formerly been intimately connected with some highly respectable ministers among the dissenters, and retained a cordial regard for many to the last. He considered the strong prejudices which attach to both Churchmen and Dissenters, as arising more from education than from principle. But, being himself both a clergyman and an incumbent in the Church of England, he wished to be consist ent. In public, therefore, he felt he could not act with some ministers, whom he thought truly good men, and to whom he cordially wished success in their endeavors; and he patiently met the consequence. They called him a *bigot,* and he, in return, prayed for them, that they might not be *really* such.

He had formerly taken much pains in composing his sermons, as I could perceive in one MS. which I looked through: and, even latterly, I have known him, whenever he felt it necessary, produce admirable plans for the pulpit. I own I thought his judgment deficient, in not deeming such preparation necessary at *all* times. I have sat in pain, when he has spoken unguardedly in this way before young ministers; men, who, with but comparatively slight degrees of his information and experience, would draw encouragement to ascend the pulpit with but little previous study of their subject. A minister is not to be blamed, who cannot rise to qualifications which some of his brethren have attained; but he is certainly bound to improve his own talent to the utmost of his power: he is not to cover his sloth, his love of company, or his disposition to attend a wealthy patron, with the *pretence* of depending entirely on *divine influence.* Timothy had as good ground, at least, for expecting such influence as any of his successors in the ministry; and yet the apostle admonishes him to *give attendance to reading, to exhortation*, and *to doctrine*—to *neglect not the gift that* was *in* him—to *meditate upon these things*—to *give* himself WHOLLY *to them, that* his *profiting* might *appear to all*.

Mr. Newton regularly preached on the Sunday morning and evening at St. Mary Woolnoth, and also on the Wednesday morning. After he was turned of seventy he often undertook to assist other clergymen; sometimes, even to the preaching of six sermons in the space of a week. What was more extraordinary, he continued his usual course of preaching at his own church after he was fourscore years old, and that, when he could no longer see to read his text! His memory and voice sometimes failed him; but it was remarked, that, at this great age, he was nowhere more collected or lively than in the pulpit. He was punctual as to time with his congregation. Every first Sunday evening in the month he preached on relative duties. Mr. Alderman Lea regularly sent his carriage to convey him to the church, and Mr. Bates sent his servant to attend him in the pulpit; which friendly assistance was continued till Mr. Newton could appear no longer in public.

His ministerial visits were exemplary. I do not recollect one, though favored with many, in which his general information and lively genius did not communicate instruction, and his affectionate and condescending sympathy did not leave comfort.

Truth demands it should be said, that he did not always administer consolation, nor give an account of characters, with sufficient discrimination. His talent did not lie in *discerning of spirits.* I never saw him so much moved, as when any friend endeavored to correct his errors in this respect. His credulity seemed to arise from the consciousness he had of his own integrity; and from that sort of parental fondness which he bore to all his friends, real or pretended. I knew one, since dead, whom he thus described, while living—"He is certainly an odd man, and has his failings; but he has great integrity, and I hope he is going to heaven:" whereas, almost all who knew him thought the man should go first into the pillory!

In his FAMILY, Mr. Newton might be admired more safely than imitated. His excessive attachment to Mrs. Newton is so fully displayed in his "Narrative," and confirmed in the two volumes he thought it proper to publish, entitled, "Letters to a Wife," that the reader will need no information on this subject. Some of his friends wished this violent attachment had been cast more into the shade; as tending to furnish a spur, where human nature generally needs a curb. He used, indeed, to speak of such attachments, in the abstract, as *idolatry;* though his own was providentially ordered to be the main hinge on which his preservation and deliverance turned, while in his worst state. Good men, however, cannot be too cautious how they give sanction, by their expressions or example, to a passion, which, when not under sober regulation, has overwhelmed not only families, but states, with disgrace and ruin.

With his unusual degree of benevolence and affection, it was not extraordinary that the spiritual interests of his servants were brought forward, and examined severally every Sunday afternoon: nor that, being treated like children, they should grow old in his service. In short, Mr. Newton could *live* no longer than he could *love:* it is no wonder, therefore, if his nieces had more of his heart than is generally afforded to their own children by the fondest parents. It has already been mentioned that his house was an asylum for the perplexed or afflicted. Young ministers were peculiarly the objects of his attention: he instructed them; he encouraged them; he warned them; and might truly be said to be a father in Christ, *spending and being spent*, for the interest of his church. In order thus to execute the various avocations of the day, he used to rise early: he seldom was found abroad in the evening, and was exact in his appointments.

Of his WRITINGS, I think little needs to be said here; they are in wide circulation, and best speak for themselves.

The " Sermons" which Mr. Newton published at Liverpool, after being refused on his first application for orders, were intended to show what he would have preached, had he been admitted: they are highly creditable to his understanding and to his heart. The facility with which he attained so much of the learned languages seems partly accounted for, from his being able to acquire so early, a neat and natural style in his own language, and that under such evident disadvantages. His " Review of Ecclesiastical History," so far as it proceeded, has been much esteemed; and, if it had done no more than excite the Rev. Joseph Milner (as that most valuable and instructive author informs us it did) to pursue Mr. Newton's idea more largely, it was sufficient success. Before this, the world seems to have lost sight of a history of real christianity; and to have been content with what, for the most part, was but an account of the ambition and politics of secular men assuming the christian name.

It must be evident to any one who observes the spirit of all his Sermons, Hymns, Tracts, &c. that nothing is aimed at which should be met by critical investigation. In the preface to his Hymns, he remarks, " Though I would not offend readers of taste by a wilful coarseness and negligence, I do not write professedly for them. I have simply declared my own views and feelings, as I might have done if I had composed hymns in some of the newly discovered islands in the South Sea, where no person had any knowledge of the name of Jesus but myself."

To dwell, therefore, with a critical eye on this part of his public character would be absurd and impertinent: it would be to erect a tribunal to which he seems not amenable. He appears to have paid no regard to a nice ear, or an accurate reviewer; but preferring a style at once neat and perspicuous, to have laid out himself entirely for the service of the Church of God, and more especially for the tried and experienced part of its members.

His chief excellence, as a writer, seemed to lie in the easy and natural style of his epistolary correspondence. His letters will be read while real religion exists; and they are the best draught of his own mind.

He had so largely communicated with his friends in this way, that I have heard him say, he thought if his letters were collected they would make several folios. He selected many of these for publication; and expressed a hope that no other person would take that liberty with the rest, which were so widely spread abroad. In this, however, he was disappointed and grieved; as he once remarked to me: and for which reason I do not annex any letters that I received from him. He esteemed that collection published under the title of " Cardiphonia," as the most useful of his writings, and mentioned various instances of the benefits which he heard they had conveyed to many.

His " Apologia," or defence of conformity, was written on occasion of some reflections (perhaps only jocular) cast on him at that time. His "Letters to a Wife," written during his three voyages to Africa, and published in 1793, have been received with less satisfaction than most of his other writings. While, however, his advanced age and inordinate fondness may be pleaded for this publication, care should be taken lest men fall into a contrary extreme; and suppose *that* temper to be their *wisdom*, which leads them to avoid another, which they consider as his *weakness*. But his "Messiah," before mentioned, his Letters of the Rev. Mr. Vanlier, Chaplain at the Cape—his Memoirs of the Rev. John Cowper, (brother to the poet,) and those of the Rev. Mr. Grimshaw, of Yorkshire, together with his single sermons and tracts, have been well received, and will remain a public benefit.

I recollect reading a MS. which Mr. Newton lent me, containing a correspondence that had passed between himself and the Rev. Dr. Dixon, Principal of St. Edmund Hall, Oxford; and another MS. of a correspondence between him and the late Rev. Martin Madan. They would have been very interesting to the public, particularly the latter; and were striking evidences of Mr. Newton's humility, piety and faithfulness: but reasons of delicacy led him to commit the whole to the flames.

To speak of his writings in the mass, they certainly possess what many have aimed at, but very few attained, namely, *originality*. They are the language of the heart: they show a deep experience of its religious feelings; a continual anxiety to sympathize with man in his wants, and to direct him to his only resources.

His CONVERSATION and familiar habits with his friends were more peculiar, amusing and instructive, than any I ever witnessed. It is difficult to convey a clear idea of them by description. I venture, therefore, to add a few pages of what I may call his *Table-Talk*, which I took down at different times, both in company and in private, from his lips. Such a collection of printed remarks will not have so much point, as when spoken in connection with the occasions that produced them: they must appear to considerable disadvantage, thus detached; and candid allowance should be made by the reader on this account. They, however, who had the privilege of Mr. Newton's conversation when living, cannot but recognise the speaker in most of them, and derive both profit and pleasure from these remains of their late valuable friend; and such as had not, will (if I do not mistake) think them the most valuable part of this book.

~~~~~~~~~~~~~~

REMARKS

MADE BY MR. NEWTON IN FAMILIAR CONVERSATION

While the mariner uses the loadstone, the philosopher may attempt to investigate the cause; but after all, in steering through the ocean, he can make no other use of it than the mariner.

If an angel were sent to find the most perfect man, he would probably not find him composing a body of divinity, but perhaps a cripple in a poor house, whom the parish wish dead, and humbled before God with far lower thoughts of himself than others have of him.

When a christian goes into the world because he sees it is his *call*, yet, while he feels it also his *cross*, it will not hurt him.

Satan will seldom come to a christian with a gross temptation: a green log and a candle may be safely left together; but bring a few shavings, then some small sticks, and then larger, and you may soon bring the green log to ashes.

If two angels were sent from heaven to execute a divine command, one to conduct an empire, and the other to sweep a street in it, they would feel no inclination to change employments.

What some call providential openings are often powerful temptations; the heart, in wandering, cries, Here is a way opened before me:—but, perhaps, not to be *trodden* but *rejected*.

I should have thought mowers very idle people; but they work while they whet their scythes. Now devotedness to God, whether it mows or whets the scythe, still goes on with the work.

A christian should never plead spirituality for being a sloven; if he be but a shoe-cleaner, he should be the best in the parish.

My course of study, like that of a surgeon, has principally consisted in walking the hospital.

My principal method of defeating heresy, is by establishing truth. One proposes to fill a bushel with *tares;* now if I can fill it first with *wheat*, I shall defy his attempts.

When *some* people talk of religion, they mean they have heard so many sermons, and performed so many devotions, and thus mistake the *means* for the *end*. But true religion is an habitual re-collection of God and intention to serve him, and this turns every thing into gold. We are apt to suppose that we need something splendid to evince our devotion, but true devotion equals things—washing plates and cleaning shoes is a high office, if performed in a right spirit. If three angels were sent to earth, they would feel per-fect indifference who should perform the part of prime minister, parish minister, or watchman.

When a ship goes to sea, among a vast variety of its articles and circumstances, there is but one object regarded, namely, doing the business of the voyage: every bucket is employed with respect to *that*.

Many have puzzled themselves about the ori-gin of evil; I observe there *is* evil, and that there is a way to escape it, and with this I begin and end.

Consecrated things under the law were first sprinkled with blood, and then anointed with oil, and thenceforward were no more common. Thus under the Gospel, every christian has been a common vessel for profane purposes; but when sprinkled with the blood of Christ, and anointed by God the Father, (2 Cor. 1 : 21,) he becomes separated and consecrated to God.

I would not give a straw for that assurance which sin will not damp. If David had come from his adultery, and had talked of his assurance at that time, I should have despised his speech.

A spirit of adoption is the spirit of a child; he may disoblige his father, yet he is not afraid of being turned out of doors: the *union* is not dissolved, though the *communion* is. He is not well with his father, therefore must be unhappy, as their interests are inseparable.

We often seek to apply cordials when the patient is not prepared for them, and it is the patient's advantage, that he cannot take a medicine when prematurely offered. When a man comes to me and says, "I am quite happy," I am not sorry to find him come again with some fears. I never saw a work stand well without a check. "I only want," says one, "to be sure of being safe, and then I will go on." No; perhaps, then you will go *off*.

For an old christian to say to a young one, "Stand in my evidence," is like a man who has with difficulty climbed by a ladder or scaffolding to the top of the house, and cries to one at the bottom, "This is a place for a prospect—come up at a step."

A christian in the world is like a man who has had a long intimacy with one, whom at length he finds out to have been the murderer of a kind father; the intimacy, after this, will surely be broken.

"Except a man be born again, he cannot see the kingdom of God." A man may live in a deep mine in Hungary, never having seen the light of the sun; he may have received accounts of prospects, and by the help of a candle may have examined a few engravings of them ; but let him be brought out of the mine, and set on the mountain, what a difference appears !

Candor will always allow much for inexperience. I have been thirty years forming my own views, and in the course of this time some of my hills have been sinking, and some of my valleys have risen; but how unreasonable would it be to expect all this should take place in another person, and that in the course of a year or two.

Candor forbids us to estimate a character from its accidental blots. Yet it is thus that David and others have been treated.

There is the analogy of faith : it is a master-key which not only opens particular doors, but carries you through the whole house ; but an attachment to a rigid system is dangerous. Luther once turned out the epistle of St. James, because it disturbed his system. I shall preach, perhaps, very usefully upon two seemingly opposite texts, while kept apart; but if I attempt nicely to reconcile them, it is ten to one if I don't begin to bungle.

I can conceive a living man without an arm or

leg, but not without a head or a heart ; so there are some truths essential to vital religion, and which all awakened souls are taught.

Apostacy, in all its branches, takes its rise from atheism. "I have set the Lord always before me," &c.

We are surprised at the fall of a famous professor, but, in the sight of God he was gone before ; it is only *we* that have now first discovered it. "He that despiseth small things, shall fall by little and little."

There are critical times of danger. After great services, honors and consolations, we should stand upon our guard. Noah, Lot, David, Solomon, fell in these circumstances. Satan is a footpad : a footpad will not attack a man in going to the bank, but in returning with his pocket full of money.

A christian is like a young nobleman, who, on going to receive his estate, is at first enchanted with its prospects ; this in a course of time may wear off, but a sense of the value of the estate grows daily.

When we first enter into the divine life, we propose to grow *rich ;* God's plan is to make us feel *poor.*

Good men have need to take heed of building upon groundless impressions. Mr. Whitfield had a son who, he imagined, was born to be a very extraordinary man; but the son soon died, and the father was cured of his mistake.

I remember, in going to undertake the care of a congregation, I was reading as I walked in a green lane, "Fear not, Paul, I have much people in this city." But I soon afterward was disappointed in finding that Paul was not John, and that Corinth was not Warwick.

Christ has taken our nature into heaven to represent *us;* and has left us on earth with his nature to represent *him.*

Worldly men will be true to their principles; and if we were as true to ours, the visits between the two parties would be short and seldom.

A christian in the world is like a man transacting his affairs in the rain. He will not suddenly leave his client because it rains; but the moment the business is done, he is off: as it is said in the Acts, "Being let go, they went to their own company."

God's word is certainly a restraint; but it is such a restraint as the irons which prevent children from getting into the fire.

God deals with us as we do with our children; he first *speaks*, then gives a gentle *stroke*, at last a *blow*.

The religion of a sinner stands on two pillars namely, what Christ did for us in his flesh, and what he performs in us by his Spirit. Most errors arise from an attempt to separate these two.

Man is not taught any thing to purpose till God becomes his teacher, and then the glare of the world is put out, and the value of the soul rises in full view. A man's present sentiments may not be accurate, but we make too much of sentiments. We pass a field with a few blades, we call it a field of wheat; but here is no wheat; no, not in perfection, but wheat is sown, and full ears may be expected.

Contrivers of sytems on the earth are like contrivers of systems in the heavens; where the sun and moon keep the same course in spite of the philosophers.

I endeavor to walk through the world as a physician goes through Bedlam: the patients make a noise, pester him with impertinence, and hinder him in his business; but he does the best he can, and so gets through.

A man always in society is one always on the spend; on the other hand, a mere solitary is at his best but a candle in an empty room.

If we were upon the watch for improvement, the common news of the day would furnish it; the falling of the tower in Siloam, and the slaughter of the Galileans, were the news of the day which our Lord improved.

The generality make out their righteousness by comparing themselves with some others whom they think worse; thus a woman of the town, who was in the Lock Hospital, was offended at a minister speaking to her as a sinner, because she had never picked a pocket.

Take away a toy from a child and give him another, and he is satisfied; but if he be hungry, no toy will do. Thus, as new-born babes, true believers desire the sincere milk of the word; and the desire of grace in this way is grace.

One said that the great saints in the calendar were many of them poor sinners; Mr. Newton replied they were poor saints indeed, if they did not feel that they were great sinners.

A wise man looks upon men as he does upon horses, and considers their caparisons of title, wealth and place, but as harness.

The force of what we deliver from the pulpit is often lost by a starched, and what is frequently called a correct style; and, especially, by adding meretricious ornaments. I called upon a lady who had been robbed, and she gave me a striking account of the fact; but had she put it into heroics, I should neither so well have understood her, nor been so well convinced that she had been robbed.

When a man says he received a blessing under a sermon, I begin to inquire the character of the man who speaks of the help he has received

The Roman people proved the effect they received under a sermon of Antony, when they flew to avenge the death of Cæsar.

The Lord has reason far beyond our ken, for opening a wide door while he stops the mouth of a useful preacher. John Bunyan would not have done half the good he did if he had remained preaching in Bedford instead of being shut up in Bedford prison.

If I could go to France, and give every man in it a right and peaceable mind by my labor, I should have a statue: but, to produce such an effect in the conversion of one soul, would be a far greater achievement.

Ministers would over-rate their labors, if they did not think it worth while to be born, and spend ten thousand years in labor and contempt, to recover one soul.

Do not tell me of your feelings. A traveller would be glad of fine weather, but if he be a man of business, he will go on. Bunyan says, You must not judge of a man's haste by his horse, for when the horse can hardly move you may see, by the rider's urging him, what a hurry he is in.

A man and a beast may stand upon the same mountain, and even touch one another; yet they are in two different worlds: the beast perceives nothing but the grass; but the man contemplates the prospect, and thinks of a thousand remote

things. Thus a christian may be solitary at a full
exchange: he can converse with the people there
upon trade, politics and the stocks; but they
cannot talk with him upon *the peace of God which
passeth all understanding*.

It is a mere fallacy to talk of the sins of a short
life. The sinner is always a sinner. Put a pump
into a river, you may throw out some water, but
the river remains.

Professors who own the doctrines of free
grace, often act inconsistently with their own
principles when they are angry at the defects
of others.

We should take care that we do not make our
profession of religion a receipt in full for all other
obligations. A man truly illuminated will no more
despise others than Bartimeus, after his own eyes
were opened, would take a stick and beat every
blind man he met.

We much mistake, in supposing that the removal of a particular objection would satisfy the
objector. Suppose I am in bed, and want to know
whether it be light, it is not enough if I draw
back the curtain; for though there be light, I
must have eyes to see it.

Too deep a consideration of eternal realities
might unfit a man for his present circumstances.
Walking through St. Bartholomew's Hospital, or
Bedlam, must deeply affect a feeling mind; but,

in reality, this world is a far worse scene. It has but two wards: in the one, men are miserable, in the other, mad.

Some preachers near Olney dwelt on the doctrine of predestination: an old woman said—Ah! I have long settled that point: for, if God had not chosen me before I was born, I am sure he would have seen nothing in me to have chosen me for afterwards.

I see the unprofitableness of controversy in the case of Job and his friends: for, if God had not interposed, had they lived to this day, they would have continued the dispute.

It is pure mercy that negatives a particular request. A miser would pray very earnestly for gold, if he believed prayer would gain it; whereas, if Christ had any favor to him he would take his gold away. A child walks in the garden in spring, and sees cherries; he knows they are good fruit, and therefore asks for them. "No, my dear," says the father, "they are not yet ripe; stay till the season."

If I cannot take pleasure in infirmities, I can sometimes feel the profit of them. I can conceive a king to pardon a rebel, and take him into his family, and then say, "I appoint you for a season to wear a fetter. At a certain season I will send a messenger to knock it off. In the mean time this fetter will serve to remind you of your state; it may humble you and restrain you from rambling."

Some christians, at a glance, seem of superior order; and are not: they want a certain quality. At a florist's feast the other day, a certain flower was determined to bear the bell; but it was found to be an artificial flower: there is a quality called GROWTH which it had not.

Doctor Taylor, of Norwich, said to me, "Sir, I have collated every word in the Hebrew Scriptures seventeen times; and it is very strange if the doctrine of atonement, which you hold, should not have been found by me." I am not surprised at this: I once went to light my candle with the extinguisher on it: now, prejudices from education, learning, &c. often form an extinguisher. It is not enough that you bring the candle: you must remove the extinguisher.

I measure ministers by square measure. I have no idea of the size of a table, if you only tell me how *long* it is; but, if you also say how *wide*, I can tell its dimensions. So, when you tell me what a man is in the pulpit, you must also tell me what he is out of it, or I shall not know his size.

A man should be *born* to high things not to lose himself in them. Slaters will walk on the ridge of a house with ease, which would turn our heads.

Much depends on the way we come into trouble. Paul and Jonah were both in a storm, but in very different circumstances.

I have read of many wicked Popes, but the worst Pope I ever met with is POPE SELF.

The men of this world are children. Offer a child an apple and a bank note, he will doubtless choose the apple.

The heir of a great estate, while a child, thinks more of a few shillings in his pocket than of his inheritance. So a christian is often more elated by some frame of heart than by his title to glory.

A dutiful child is ever looking forward to the holidays, when he shall return to his father; but he does not think of running from school before.

The Gospel is a proclamation of free mercy to guilty creatures—an act of grace to rebels. Now, though a rebel should throw away his pistols, and determine to go into the woods, and make his mind better before he goes to court and pleads the act; he may, indeed, not be found in *arms*, yet, being taken in his reforming scheme, he will be hanged.

Man is made capable of three births: by nature, he enters into the present world; by grace, into spiritual light and life; by death, into glory.

In my imagination, I sometimes fancy I could make a perfect minister. I take the eloquence of ——, the knowledge of ——, the zeal of ——, and the pastoral meekness, tenderness and piety of —— : then, putting them all together into one man, I say to myself, "*This* would be a perfect minister." Now there is one, who, if he choose it, could actually *do* this; but he never did. He has seen fit to do otherwise, and to divide these gifts *to every man severally as he will.*

I feel like a man who has no money in his pocket, but is allowed to draw for all he wants upon one infinitely rich; I am, therefore, at once both a beggar and a rich man.

I went one day to Mrs. G——'s just after she had lost all her fortune; I could not be surprised to find her in tears, but she said, "I suppose you think I am crying for my loss, but that is not the case: I am now weeping to think I should feel so much uneasiness on this account." After that I never heard her speak again upon the subject as long as she lived.

I have many books that I cannot sit down to read: they are, indeed, good and sound; but, like halfpence, there goes a great quantity to a little amount. There are *silver* books; and a very few *golden* books: but I have one book worth more than all, called the Bible; and that is a book of *bank notes.*